Acknowledgements

In producing this collection of Exercises, I have been indebted to many people in Industry, Commerce and Education who have helped me by sharing their experience, giving me ideas, commenting on my draft efforts, and evaluating the materials in school.

Two major companies have been particularly helpful and generous. Rowntree Mackintosh plc, chiefly in the persons of their Public Relations Director, Gavin Russell, and Management Training Manager, Chris Parkin, but also through several of their colleagues, has given me unlimited advice and contacts. The same has been true of I.C.I. Agricultural Division, and I am especially grateful to its Personnel Director, Hector McLean, Career Development Manager, Ray Turner, and former employees Alan Barton and Barry Lee. Another former employee, Tony Brennan, himself a genuine expert in the production of experiential exercises, has spent hours reading, watching, commenting on and suggesting modifications to the exercises and the text, all of which have substantially improved the quality of the content. I would also like to mention John Brand (Television and Radio Techniques), Michael Browning (ex - STC), Aubrey Watson (Watson, Lane and Keane), Stephen Williams (English Heritage) and Bill Wright (Teesside Industrial Mission).

From the world of Education, I have been greatly helped by Jim Jordan of North Yorkshire Education Authority and Harold Heller, Chief Adviser, and several of his colleagues in Cleveland. Bertie Everard of the University of London Institute of Education and John McGuiness of the School of Education at Durham University have always been available for advice. And colleagues in schools and colleges throughout the North of England have been most generous in giving me their time, particularly in the evaluation of the exercises. If I single out Mollie Haigh, Carole Wood, and Norman Barton from my own school, Easingwold; Kate Brown (South Park 6th Form College), Tony Milnes (Langbaurgh School) and a number of colleagues from De Brus School, all in Cleveland; and Peggy Hooton (Biddick School), Ken Shenton (Harton School) and several colleagues from Monkseaton High School, all in the former Tyne and Wear, it is only because they have done more than others.

Finally, I must thank my own Governors and Authority for granting me secondment and the School of Education at the University of Newcastle upon Tyne for making me so welcome. Bill Dennison has supervised my studies most purposefully, using his own enthusiasm for experiential learning to stimulate and encourage my efforts. And the secretarial staff, Maureen O'Driscoll and her colleague Pam Lauder, have been remarkably tolerant to the many demands I have made upon their time and skills. They have been unfailingly cheerful in typing, revising and reproducing the thousands of sheets involved in several drafts, and have kept me going by their obvious interest in and commitment to the work I had undertaken.

Roger Kirk
June 1986

Learning
in Action

*Activities for personal
and group development*

Roger Kirk

Basil Blackwell

For Christine - who is!

© Roger Kirk 1987

First published 1987
Published by Basil Blackwell Limited
108 Cowley Road
Oxford OX4 1JF
England

British Library Cataloguing in Publication Data
Kirk, Roger
  Learning in action : activities for
  personal and group development.
  1. Social skills—Study and teaching
  I. Title
  302'07   HM299

  ISBN 0–631–90123–X

Typeset in 11pt Plantin
by Oxprint Ltd, Oxford
Printed in Great Britain
by Bell and Bain Ltd, Glasgow

Contents

PART 1

The Framework

Introduction

During a recent discussion with a friend about the comparability of management in industry and education, he said that in his work as an industrial manager he concentrated on changing one thing at a time while it appeared that education was engaged in changing most things all of the time. I took his point, though it is only fair to say that for those of us who work in schools, a good many of the changes, in which we seem permanently to be involved, are not of our own volition.

The circumstances under which I took up my first Headship in Teesside in 1973 could hardly have provided a better example of this. My appointment coincided with the advent of comprehensive education and the reorganisation of schools locally, and I was entrusted with the merging of three secondary modern schools with a first year comprehensive intake. Unfinished buildings meant we were on three sites, linked by a double-decker bus on permanent hire, and insufficient planning time prevented us from even having a total staff meeting before the school opened. 1973 was also the year in which the school leaving age was raised from 15 to 16, giving us a group of extremely unwilling and disaffected senior pupils. Local government reorganisation was to follow the next year, so there was considerable uncertainty among politicians and officers; it was only three years, in any case, since Teesside had previously been reorganised.

Into this daunting scene of confusion stepped the unlikely figure of the Senior Chaplain of Teesside Industrial Mission. He made contact with all the new Heads in Stockton, offering us the opportunity of sitting down at regular intervals with managers of comparable responsibility from the Agricultural Division of ICI in Billingham. These meetings offered three things: the opportunity for 'ventilation' over a decent lunch away from school (very welcome in those early days); some training in management skills; and a consultancy service for our schools.

I was one of those who accepted this offer with alacrity. Three managers were involved in the early stages, all subsequently to become personal friends; they were most helpful in monitoring, at our invitation, the communication network and meetings procedures of the school. They also introduced me to the whole concept of organisation development, and gave me my first learning in management skills. It was in this context that I encountered a structured and systematic approach to experiential learning for the first time. As a contrast to the directive style of teaching which I had received in my school days and which I used in my own classroom, we learnt from exercises, simulations and experiences. This action mode was balanced by a reflective mode in which the learning was reinforced, and I then attempted to apply the skills I was starting to acquire in school. Areas covered included communication, delegation, use of time, decision making, team building and so on.

One of the ICI trainers involved was also a parent of a pupil in the school, and well known to the staff because of his involvement in many of our activities. He was asked by members of staff about the work he was doing with myself and other Heads, and the interest that they showed led to the establishment of our own staff development programme. This programme covered similar ground and used identical methods to those employed in the Heads' development programme, and did much for the skills of the staff involved and for the general effectiveness and atmosphere of the school.

It was not long before the effects were seen in the classroom. Teachers realised that the experiential methods through which they had learnt so much and the skills which these techniques were designed to convey were equally important for the children. This affected their own teaching style and also encouraged them to use visitors from industry and elsewhere to introduce some of these exercises into the classroom. At this stage the focus was mainly on furthering the skills and attitudes which would be vital to young people if they were to be able to play a full part in adult life, either in or out of work.

In 1981 I was appointed to the Headship of Easingwold School in North Yorkshire. Although the school and its catchment area were entirely different, again I was lucky enough to inherit a dedicated and imaginative staff, and soon found that the concept of staff and pupil development and the medium of experiential learning were equally relevant. A substantial proportion of the staff joined in one or more elements of the development programme, which was devised to increase levels of professional skill and competence and to enhance management effectiveness. The programme on this occasion was supported by Rowntree Mackintosh with the same commitment and expertise as ICI had demonstrated for its predecessor. Once again the programme had its effects in the classroom, and the school now has a course for all pupils in years 1 to 5 called *You and Your World*, which aims to equip young people for the world outside school. Much of the work involved is of the experiential variety, and this type of learning has extended into the sixth form induction course and into the CPVE course which the school embraced at its inception in 1985.

We soon found that as this work extended we were short of suitable materials to use for experiential learning. Most of our existing materials were the exercises to which we had been introduced by ICI and Rowntree Mackintosh and these were being over-used. Perhaps more important than that, they were unsuitable in a number of other ways. Some required more time than was available in the single or double lesson which the *You and Your World* course allowed or in the evening sessions of the staff development programme. Many presupposed a far larger trainer commitment than the one or two teachers to a class of 30–35, which was our ratio. Some involved expensive (by our standards) or elaborate resources. Very few were suitable for use with the academically least able, as they generally demanded a reasonable facility in reading and writing. And, when it came to work with staff, many were based in an industrial setting, which often seemed irrelevant to educational needs and which gave ammunition to the cynics who questioned the validity of the whole operation.

At this point I was lucky enough to be offered secondment by North Yorkshire Education Authority to take up a Teacher Fellowship for two terms at the School of Education of Newcastle University. My aim was to produce a collection of materials for use with pupils of all ages and abilities and in the staff development programme at Easingwold School. Some of these exercises would be based in a school setting (some were actually suggested to me by members of staff); they would all take account of the time that we had available for work of this kind; they would be sparing in the use of teacher and other resources; and they would include material specifically aimed at those with learning difficulties. I am conscious that this last aim has only been very partially fulfilled.

It is thanks to the encouragement and support of Dr Dennison of the School of Education at Newcastle, and of many other colleagues both in education and in industry, whose help is acknowledged separately, that these exercises are now to reach a wider audience than was originally conceived.

For reasons of simplicity (with no sexist implications) teachers and children alike are referred to by the masculine pronoun.

1

Why experiential learning?

I first became fully aware of the power and significance of experiential learning some twenty years ago, when, as a lecturer in a College of Education I was involved for a number of years in experimental work with less-able 14–15-year-old boys from a local secondary modern school. Together with a group of students I spent periods of a week under canvas on the moors with these youngsters, during which time they were able, to a large extent, to plan their own work and research. They lived and studied in small groups, supported by the most up-to-date equipment we could lay our hands on at the time. They accepted considerable responsibility both for creating their own programme and for running the camp site, and we tried to allow them to experience the wealth of opportunities—social, physical and academic—which the moors provided.

The results were highly gratifying and certainly had a major impact on my own educational thinking. I remember two particular incidents. One was the comment made by one boy at the end of the week that it was the first time he had learned anything which seemed to him fresh and new; everything else had been 'washed through hundreds of minds'. The other was where a boy, starved of success at school, suddenly discovered that he could create a niche for himself as the expert washer-up. He defended this role vigorously against all comers. It may not have made for the quickest or most efficient washing-up, but it did wonders for his self-esteem!

The difference between traditional and experiential learning

It may be helpful here to give a brief description of the major differences between traditional and experiential styles of learning. Without wishing to be dismissive of or to caricature the way in which so many of us were taught in the past, it is likely to have been teacher-centred, didactic, directive, corrective and mostly concerned with the acquisition of knowledge in well-defined subject areas. By contrast, experiential learning is skills-based as opposed to knowledge-based, and the teacher acts as facilitator rather than instructor; it is grounded in a mutual respect between teacher and learner.

Another important feature of the experiential mode of learning is that it is open-ended and cross-curricular rather than subject-based. Students are encouraged to programme themselves as far as possible, to experiment and to discover; learning is more to do with questions than with answers.

Much of the work is done in groups because it is through working with others that an awareness of relationships can best be acquired. The ability to work with others and to participate in decision making and problem solving is developed through learning of this kind, as are the skills of listening and communicating. A feeling of responsibility for the group will grow, and participants can be encouraged to learn how to evaluate the performance both of the group and of themselves as individuals. They will realise that evaluation is not a negative concept like criticism and that true responsibility welcomes feed-back and is not inhibited by the fear of blame. In fact, as experiential learning is process-based and not content-based, students will discover that the 'how' of learning is at least as important as the 'what', if not more so.

Finally, experiential learning lays equal emphasis on the cognitive and affective domains. Emotional development grows alongside the acquisition of knowledge, and this personal growth leads to heightened self-awareness and a greater self-confidence. With maturity comes a deeper sensitivity to and concern for the emotional and physical needs of others, and the ability to acknowledge one's shortcomings without guilt. In short, there is a totality of learning which traditional methods have never been able to provide.

A model of experiential learning

The Development Training Advisory Group (DTAG) has devised a model which shows experiential learning as a process involving active learning as opposed to passive teaching. It is a model which stresses the *process* of the learning rather than its content—'Now, how did that happen?'. People learn by doing things in a group, reviewing how they worked together, drawing conclusions and applying these to their real-life experiences elsewhere (Figure 1). Experiential learning is concerned with the systematic and purposeful development of the whole person. It is the only sort of learning as a result of which people change. It is a source of confidence, flexibility, awareness and maturity of emotion, and it helps provide the ability to handle unknown situations.

Figure 1

The model applied
This book makes use of the model by encouraging students to participate in activities intended to place them quickly and simply in situations in which they can learn about their abilities, feelings and impact on other people. For example, exercises such as *The Orange*

7

Market and *Family Business* are designed to make students aware of, and more knowledgeable in, presentation skills. They could appropriately be used by young people preparing to attend an interview. By reviewing the exercise after its completion, the participants identify skills that will help them in real interviews and gain confidence and maturity in approaching them. Two 15-year-olds, after experiencing activities of this sort, went for their first interview practice with a hairdresser in a nearby town. This involved a bus journey and a considerable walk and it happened to be an extremely wet day. Despite all their preparations, they were a bedraggled couple when they finally arrived at the salon. The hairdresser greeted them with the comment that they needed to ' . . . well smarten themselves up' if they were going for an interview. Their subsequent evaluation of the incident was: 'We learned today that at an interview, however rude someone is to you, you have to keep your temper'. Experiential learning was working.

In a different context it is possible to structure a working environment in which experiential learning can be a constant process. For example, when young people join a youth club, membership can offer a range of new experiences. Inevitably it provides opportunities to reflect on attitudes towards money, relationships, morals, sex or whatever. Concepts are formed as a result of this reflection. Later, the implications of these concepts are tried out experimentally in new situations—both in the club and in many other inter-group and interpersonal exchanges. Testing things out leads the young people on to new experiences. The cycle starts again. Indeed, for all of us a number of learning cycles are occurring simultaneously. These, together with a combination of action and reflection, form the basis of experiential learning.

There are tensions in the process, for example, between the experience and the formulation of concepts, and between the processes of reflection and further experience. The young people gain useful experience more quickly as they learn how to learn. The youth club organiser, in this example, can arrange the environment of the club in such a way that there is opportunity both for a range of experiences and the chance to reflect.

Who is this book for?

1 The school
In school, experiential learning is already furthered through extra-curricular physical pursuits, through social service and through field work. Indeed, the growth of field work and of other experience-based forms of practical learning within the classroom in traditional academic subjects has been one of the most heartening recent educational trends, and it now seems likely that it will transform our system of examining and appraising pupils during the next decade.

There are other aspects of experiential learning, however, which are rather different, but which will have a substantial impact on the attitude of pupils and the teaching style of teachers. These often appear in a time-table or syllabus as 'Life and Social Skills', though this title has in my view acquired unfortunate overtones through its too narrow association with the vocational aspects of education, where it has an important, but not exclusive, place. The exercises contained in this book lie in this field and are particularly concerned with the *Doing*, *Reviewing* and *Learning* stages of the DTAG model (see above). It is hoped that the *Application* will follow naturally.

2 Colleges and elsewhere

Over the past few years courses aimed at the growth of skills in both personal and group development have become a much more marked feature of colleges of further education and sixth forms. Many now have an element of this kind as part of their core studies, and it is an essential component of TVEI and CPVE courses. Many of the exercises in this book are suitable for use with students of all ages, but some have been specifically designed for this particular age group and have been found to be successful. They should be equally appropriate for increasing the skills and awareness of YTS trainees, who again have a personal and group development component in their training.

3 Staff development

I first encountered experiential exercises on a staff development course presented by consultants from ICI. They were particularly helpful to me in promoting the cooperative skills of our staff team and in developing the interpersonal and managerial skills which furthered that cooperative process. I had this in mind in the production of this book, and the exercises have been used successfully (and enjoyably) with Advisers, Heads and other staff of both primary and secondary schools, as well as with TVEI trainers and student teachers.

The nature of the exercises

It may be helpful to summarise the aspects of personal and group development which these exercises are intended to encourage and develop. They can be arranged under three headings, although there is obvious overlap between them:

1 Individual skills and attitudes
- widening the concept of success
- self-respect and respect for others
- self-knowledge—appreciation of one's strengths and weaknesses
- the growth of self-confidence, maturity and responsibility
- the ability to express one's feelings, to give and receive feed-back
- the ability to listen, observe and record

2 *Group skills*

- understanding the ways groups work; the difference between task and process
- the ability to work cooperatively; to tolerate and support others and to look for their strengths
- understanding the importance of leadership; discovering different styles of leadership
- the ability to retrieve, share and communicate information

3 *'Managerial' skills*

- the ability to 'manage' everyday necessities of life
- the ability to plan, establish priorities, control time
- the ability to solve problems
- the ability to make decisions
- the skills of negotiation

It must be re-emphasised that there is considerable overlap between these categories and the exercises are designed to be used flexibly by the tutor. It is arguable, for instance, whether *Classroom Corridor* is more an exercise in group behaviour than in problem solving, or whether *The Go-Between* is more to do with communication skills, leadership styles or inter-personal skills.

Whatever the case, the skills and attitudes listed above can best be acquired, it seems to me, through the medium of experiential learning. In fact this may be the *only* way that they can be acquired in any real depth. There are excellent films, books and speakers available, but these can never have the same impact as having to work through live situations in which the need for the attitudes and abilities described above becomes apparent and through which the understanding and skills can be developed. Carefully planned and presented exercises and simulations will provide this opportunity. It is hoped that this book will help in supplying suitable exercises, which will act as vehicles to stimulate experience and behaviour capable of analysis for learning.

Experiential learning in context

A word of caution may be necessary. A teacher or trainer using experiential exercises for the first time, perhaps without much personal familiarity with them, will normally find considerable enthusiasm and enjoyment among the participants. For example, pupils may still be talking about them long after a lesson has ended. It is tempting, therefore, to make each lesson or session an occasion of experiential learning, to concentrate on the exercises themselves rather than on the learning to be gained from them. From time to time one meets teachers and lecturers intent solely on finding new 'games' (the word itself is significant), with little thought for the aims of the total learning package or even of the individual exercises themselves. Any course aimed at enhancing individual group and managerial skills and attitudes must be meticulously planned, with well-defined aims and objectives. The exercises to be used must be those which will contribute to the fulfilment of these aims and objectives, and in any case will only be one means by which the learning will be transmitted. They will be complementary to other teaching approaches being used, and will often require their own support material or follow-up reading. For example, an exercise to stimulate thought and discussion about the strengths and relevance of different styles of leadership will require a supporting input from the tutor of this topic. Such material is not included in this book, except in very limited form.

Creating the right climate

It is possible for one or two staff working on their own to undertake the responsibility for introducing individual, group and managerial skills to a school or college, using the medium of experiential learning. A department can certainly do so, but a single individual will find it extremely difficult. It is obviously more effective when this responsibility is part of the aims of the school or college as a whole, and is shared by the widest possible range of staff. This is becoming increasingly common. Many schools now have work of this kind as part of the core curriculum for all age groups, often furthered by materials designed by such bodies as the Counselling and Careers Development Unit (CCDU) at Leeds or Active Tutorial Work (ATW) at Lancaster. This trend has been encouraged by statements from the DES; and by the inclusion of such work in the syllabi for TVEI and CPVE and in the activities of the Youth Training Scheme. However, both the content of the material and the medium of experiential learning can seem irrelevant and threatening to many members of staff. It is a break with the tradition in which they have been brought up. It involves a different atmosphere, and a level of movement, bustle and noise frequently associated with lack of discipline. Students acquire the ability to discuss their feelings openly and dispassionately, and may expect staff to do likewise. And the growth of confidence among younger members of a school may seem to some to border on impertinence. It is reported that one elder statesman on the staff was particularly put out to find younger pupils greeting him with a warm 'Good morning' in the corridor after their introduction to Active Tutorial Work!

This threat can be lessened if the Head or Principal is committed to the development of this work, and if there is adequate staff training available. A lack of interest by the senior staff can be particularly damaging, and it is hoped that all Education Authorities are bringing to the attention of these staff the importance of new educational developments. Certainly the recent drive to improve the managerial skills of Heads and Principals through in-service training means that they are more likely to be familiar with the concept of experiential learning and may well have used it for their own development.

Staff training is a prerequisite for the successful introduction of this work and its accompanying teaching methods to the curriculum. If experiential learning is an integral part of a well planned and structured staff development programme, aimed at helping teachers to enhance their own understanding and inter-personal and other skills and to manage change more effectively, then the transmission of similar attitudes and activities to the classroom will follow naturally, and the whole culture of the institution will be affected. It will have its effect also on such activities as the staff induction course and departmental meetings, and certainly should be included in initial teacher training. As mentioned earlier, it was through my own involvement in staff development programmes that I came to realise the importance of giving students as well as teachers the opportunity to acquire individual, group and managerial skills. And it was because the experiential materials we used were, for the most part, so easily interchangeable between work with staff and with students that the concept of a handbook, which would contain exercises usable by both, arose.

Introducing experiential learning to the curriculum

The ethos of further and higher education and of schemes such as YTS should mean that there will be no great difficulty in introducing experiential learning of this type in such areas. There may, however, be schools where work of this kind is totally unfamiliar and where the curriculum is excessively exam-orientated. The problem then arises of *how* to introduce the approach.

If there is no slot such as 'Life and Social Skills' into which the work can easily be fitted, it may be necessary to enlist the support and help of Careers, Drama and English teachers, senior pastoral staff and form tutors. It should not be difficult to persuade them of the relevance of experiential learning, especially if they can be involved in similar work in a staff development programme. Once experiential activities are established in one or more of these areas, it will be surprising if other colleagues do not want to know more about them, with a view, possibly, to using them in their own teaching. The process of generation is then under way. Sadly, however, it must be accepted that there will always be a minority of staff who will see no value in experiential learning.

The help available from outside

As I explained in the Introduction, my own first experience in the learning of managerial skills in a formal way came from industry, and it was to industry, in conjuction with the Teesside Industrial Mission, that we looked for advice as to the organisational development of the school and for assistance in establishing our staff development programme. Much of this help is still available for work with both staff and students—and for experiential work in particular. A mass of expertise exists in the local community, and in my experience people are only too willing to help if approached. Many of them are parents or governors or have links with the institution anyway, and the fact that they generally have no role within the educational hierarchy means that they are often more acceptable to both staff and students.

The first approach to industry is often best made through the personnel/training manager (or educational manager, if it has one) of any important local firm, but a personal contact with anyone known to the school or college is often equally, or even more, effective. An Industrial Mission, if there is one in your area, is another means of access, and can frequently offer helpful exertise in its own right. The Education, Psychology and Business Studies Departments of universities, polytechnics and colleges of higher education are valuable sources of help, and may include specialist units such as CCDU (see p 11). Counselling agencies such as the Samaritans and Marriage Guidance often contain individuals skilled in the experiential field, who may be prepared to give tuition or advice.

This kind of support, however, is generally only available in the short term. Ultimately local authorities, schools and colleges will need to develop their own pool of expertise, and in many areas this is already happening. Among other interesting experiments, it is encouraging to see multi-disciplinary training groups emerging. (At one time I worked in a team including an industrial consultant and a social worker which set up a development programme for the local Social Services team.) In future, many similar links may develop across professional boundaries: schools can link with industry and vice-versa, YTS trainers with schools of education, schools with the Youth Service, and so on.

The recruitment and training of adults other than teachers (AOTs) to work alongside teachers in experiential activities in the classroom is another welcome development. Their varied and different backgrounds can introduce a wealth of experience. Moreover, they help to solve the problem, which so often obtains, of a lack of skilled observers. One trainer to 30 students is hardly a good ratio, even if some of the latter have acquired skill in observation!

Staff and students together
Given that most of the experiential materials in this book are appropriate to, and usable in, both staff development programmes

and student courses (though obviously the depth and extent of the resultant learning will vary) it is equally true that in presenting experiential learning situations to students, members of staff gain a whole range of developmental opportunities for themselves. This leads me to hope that in the not-too-distant future it may be accepted quite naturally that in experiential situations the teacher/learner distinction disappears, so that *all* become learners with the responsibility for each others' development. While the traditional school culture may make this concept difficult to realise at present, it already obtains in the more enlightened areas of FE, where older and younger learn from each other without any embarrassment.

However, the inclusion of materials which can be used interchangeably in staff development programmes, in colleges of FE and in schools, does present certain problems of nomenclature. In this book, therefore, the terms student, pupil, learner and participant are used indiscriminately to denote anyone who looks upon himself in a learning role; tutor, teacher, trainer and staff are all words describing those who are presenting the learning. As I have already suggested, in one sense they all fall into both categories anyway.

Keeping it simple

In the Introduction I explained my reasons for trying to make the exercises as simple as possible in terms of cost, manpower and time. I had in mind schools in particular, where these factors are of the essence. The situation may be different for older groups; certainly the participants will be able to draw on greater experience in encouraging each others' learning.

There is another very important reason for simplicity. The more complex an exercise becomes, the greater is the danger that the task and its successful completion will begin to dominate at the expense of the process; preoccupation with the former may obscure the learning inherent in the latter. However topical or significant the issue— whether it be the problem of redeployment, capitation, or the purchase of a pony—it is not the object of the learning. The aim of the exercises is always to highlight the *process* by which problems are solved, good decisions are made, or negotiations are effectively conducted, rather than focusing on the solution, the decision or the result of the negotiation.

2 How to use the exercises

Layout

All the exercises are presented in a similar style and consist of a cover sheet, together with the tutor's notes for the particular exercise, and the materials required by the participants. The latter are photocopiable, and may vary from several sheets to no sheets at all.

The cover sheet indicates the objectives of the exercise; a description of the activity involved; its target audience, suggested organisation, and the estimated time required; the level of tutor skill necessary to gain maximum learning; advice as to location; and the list of the materials needed for the exercise. All these are discussed in more detail later, but it must be emphasised that they are guidelines or suggestions only and can and should be adapted to suit particular needs of groups of students. Flexibility in the use of the exercises is essential as they are a means to learning, not an end in themselves.

The tutor's notes contain two elements: instructions for the conduct of the exercise, and suggestions as to some of the learning which may emerge from it. Again, these are intended to be applied with flexibility, though it is wise to maintain the basic structure and rules of the exercise. Learning may arise from almost any part of an experiential situation; even the formation of groups and the arrangement of the room, if sensitively handled, will provide significant learning opportunities.

Choosing the right exercise

Once the tutor has decided the nature of the learning to be undertaken, there are two factors to be taken into consideration in choosing an exercise: the objectives and the target audience. The objectives of each exercise are detailed on the cover sheet (a summary of these can be found on page 183). However, the skilled tutor will find uses for exercises other than those described and will realise that a good exercise can be used as a vehicle for more than one piece of learning. For instance, objectives such as the examination of group behaviour and organisation, the exploration of leadership styles, or the enhancement of communicating or listening skills can be achieved through almost any exercise. There are, however, a number of exercises in the book devised specifically to enhance observation skills. These are contained in the chapter on observation techniques (pages 29–37) as they are not considered appropriate for other uses. All the other exercises in the book can be used as a means to improve observation skills in addition to their stated objectives(s).

Recommendations as to target audience are based partly on the difficulty of the concept involved and partly on the appropriateness of the subject matter. Intellectual aptitude is far more significant than chronological age in determining which exercises will be most beneficial in providing opportunities for learning, and the tutor will wish to make choices accordingly. It is likely that the same exercise will help both bright first years and less-able third years. In mixed ability groups of the same age, the same exercise will simply provide different levels of learning.

Tutors in institutions other than schools will be able to select suitable exercises by assessing the appropriateness of the subject matter for their own students and by relating their intellectual level to the equivalent level in schools.

Organisation

Suggestions as to the organisation of the exercises cover two facets: the optimum size of the groups taking part and the amount of supervision and observation needed. Obviously the number of students in a class may make it impossible to have groups of the exact size indicated. One method of dealing with this situation is to adjust the number of observers. Alternatively tutors are recommended to examine the exercise to see if the number participating can be altered without damaging the learning outcomes or rendering the exercise impracticable. It is unlikely that the exercise can be conducted with less than the minimum group number indicated; this is certainly the case where, for example, there are five participants each with a different briefing sheet. To omit one participant and the input of his briefing sheet would render the exercise inoperable. However, it is often possible to have two participants operating from the same briefing sheet, with or without each other's knowledge. This can affect the dynamics of some exercises and even improve their learning potential. For instance, if the objective of the learning is to enhance influencing skills, what is the effect if one or two causes are promoted by two members of a group while others only have the support of one?

Estimates of the level of supervision and observation required have been based on the assumption that schools are unlikely to be able to staff a class with more than one or two teachers. If more are available (within reason), or if adults other than teachers (AOTs) are working in the school, their help will be invaluable, but the availability of such help is all too infrequent. The first thing to be done with any group of pupils being introduced to experiential learning for the first time is to ensure that they acquire the skills needed for observation. They will then be able to assist each other in learning. A special section on the introduction of observation skills at various levels has therefore been included on pages 29–37.

Timing

An attempt has been made to indicate the likely time required to use each exercise. Exercises vary from the 35 minutes of a short single lesson to two hours for a more complex afternoon or evening session. Some (eg *Evening Out, Yale Quay, Islands in the Sun*) include or demand the opportunity for some private study (or homework) and can be conveniently spread over more than one session. Timings are easily adjustable and in any case will vary once again with the age, academic ability and concentration span of individuals or groups.

Tutor skill

Included on the cover sheet of each exercise is an indication of the level of tutor skill required for those involved to derive the maximum learning. This is intended as a guide for those planning to use the work in schools or elsewhere, though I am aware that the concept of tutor skill may introduce as many problems as it seeks to solve!

The level of tutor skill is divided into three categories: A, B and C. 'A' tutors are those with considerable experience and expertise in introducing and participating in exercises of this sort and who have had some degree of past training. 'B' tutors are those who have some experience of this type of work, but who may not have had any specific training. 'C' tutors are newcomers to experiential exercises, both volunteers and pressed men or women. No assumptions are made about them other than that they are interested in the concept of experiential learning and are happy to learn the skills required to introduce it.

The exercises have been allocated to these three levels of tutor skill on the basis of three considerations:

1 The complexity of administration required for the exercise. All 'C' exercises, for example, are simple enough to require no previous experience on the part of the tutor.
2 The likely depth of learning inherent in the exercise. While a tutor who considers himself to have level 'C' skill could still tackle a level 'B' exercise, all those involved are unlikely to derive as much learning from it as they could with a more experienced tutor.
3 The risk factor—for example, the possibility that depths of feeling might be expressed during an exercise which an inexperienced tutor would be unable to handle. For this reason a 'C' tutor should not attempt an 'A' exercise.

The enhancement of tutor skills is studied in greater detail on pages 19–28.

Location

Given that the majority of exercises have to be conducted with only one tutor present, I have tried to avoid situations where groups need to be scattered in different rooms. However, groups generally do need reasonable privacy in which to work, and this can often be achieved by using a large room such as a hall, theatre or canteen; rooms with screen dividers or two adjacent rooms. Where something different is required, (eg *The Go-Between*, *Combined Operations*) this is indicated on the cover sheet. As mentioned previously, the arrangement of the furniture to provide optimum working conditions is normally part of the exercise and offers learning opportunities on its own account.

Materials

The materials required are generally simple and every effort has been made to keep costs to a minimum. Most of the materials should be available as part of the normal equipment and resources of a school or college, and of course flexibility is just as applicable in this field. For instance, *Orange Market* is equally effective as a learning medium with apples, potatoes or any equivalent fruit, vegetable or artefact!

Tutor's notes

The tutor's notes contain both the instructions for the conduct of the exercise, and indications of the main areas of learning which are likely to be covered in discussion during the *Review* session. The tutor should try to study the whole of the exercise beforehand, including all of the briefing sheets, to ascertain which aspects of the structure and rules are essential to its successful operation and which may be modified to suit particular needs. In some cases the tutor may wish to add extra briefing sheets or even to rewrite the exercise altogether.

The areas of learning which are highlighted are only some of those which will arise. It goes without saying that discussion of *any* aspect of the experiential learning will be valuable, and the depth of the student's understanding of the experience will vary according to age and intellectual ability. While it is certainly not intended that the tutor should manipulate the discussion to ensure that all the points are covered, it is important that there should be some consideration, if possible, of all the major areas of learning. For instance, in *Evening Out* both the topic of 'priorities' and that of 'influencing skills' should be included in the review.

CHAPTER

3

The enhancement of tutor skills

For experiential learning to succeed, especially among younger people, the role and skills of the tutor are enormously important. No exercise is better than the tutor who introduces it. An insensitive or inexperienced tutor can all too easily prevent learning taking place and antagonise the participants, perhaps putting them off this style of learning altogether. This chapter deals with a number of the skills which a successful tutor must have and discusses possible means of enhancing them.

Creating the right atmosphere

If experientiental learning aims to encourage participants to be open with and supportive of each other, to be less inhibited in the expression of their feelings, and to gain maturity and responsibility in planning their own learning, then the atmosphere must be conducive for them to do so. But a relaxed atmosphere without sufficient structure may actually prevent learning from taking place, especially in schools, as it can lead to a lack of self discipline among the students which will detract from a good working environment. At an early stage, therefore, the students should establish their own ground-rules and structures to ensure that everyone can get a fair hearing, that the room is arranged appropriately and speedily and so on. In working out their own ground rules in this way, they will be assuming responsibility for their own learning and growing in maturity. There is also much to learn, as has been said previously, from such a simple activity as arranging the room or forming groups, and adequate time should be allowed for this. Whatever their age or ability, participants should be encouraged to ask questions and test boundaries throughout the exercise. Far too often we and they are prepared to accept the status quo without questioning it in a positive way to see whether the situation can be made more conducive to learning and growth.

Planning the learning

It goes without saying that training in personal development must be planned and must be coherent. It is assumed that the school, college or staff group will be working to a logical programme and that different topics and exercises will be introduced at the appropriate time and not used in a random way. For instance, it is educationally unsound to fill in a spare half-hour by introducing whatever exercise comes most easily to hand, without thought or preparation. Likewise, in a programme of which experiential learning is a major element, the place for and timing of theoretical inputs must be planned with care and skill. As formal teaching is the antithesis of the experiential model, it is crucial to determine at the outset which technique is appropriate for each situation.

The presentation of an exercise is often an excellent way to introduce a new topic into the programme. The natural place for a theoretical input is after the *Review* in the learning stage of the DTAG model illustrated on page 7. It may then be helpful to use another exercise by way of reinforcement before the learning is applied to the 'for real' situation. For example, on p 8 we saw how *Family Business* could be used to introduce the topic of preparing for an interview. After theoretical inputs and work on such aspects as letters of application, the curriculum vitae and presenting oneself for interview, *Orange Market* would provide reinforcement of the learning achieved before actual interview practice takes place. In the same way, *Scramble* or *News-stand* are bound to raise the question of leadership. Either· could be followed by an input and discussion on leadership styles, using, perhaps, John Adair's well-known model of three interlocking circles. *Furniture Removers* or *Boom! Boom!* could then be used for reinforcement.

Presenting the exercise

In presenting an exercise, it is essential to take nothing for granted. If you are using an exercise for the first time, or returning to it after an interval, it is crucial to study all the sheets involved in order to be totally familiar with them. It is even better, of course, to have done the exercise yourself. This seems obvious, but in my experience it is surprising how often things can go wrong because some detail of planning or administration has been overlooked. The following points are worth remembering in preparing for the presentation of an exercise:

a *Timing* Does the exercise need to be shortened or lengthened? If so, where and how is this to be done?
b *Group size* How are the demands of the exercise to be reconciled to the likely number in the group?
c *Content* Does any of the material need re-writing? Do any briefing sheets need to be withdrawn or new ones added?
d *Rules and instructions* Are these totally clear and are you fully familiar with them?

e Location Is the room(s) you are using the correct size for the exercise?

f Materials Have you all the resources described on the cover sheet?

If any recording is necessary, is a flip-chart or blackboard available?

g Observers How many are needed? Who will fill this role?

Intervention

The quality, quantity and timing of interventions is one of the most important tutor skills and one of the hardest to acquire. It grows with experience; the more experiential learning a tutor takes part in, the more he will become aware of the value and subtlety of well-timed intervention.

In experiential learning it is the student and not the tutor who should be responsible for the learning which is taking place. This being so, the activity of the tutor should not limit, control or significantly influence the behaviour of the students, who must be allowed to reach their own solutions even if these are not the ones preferred by the tutor. So the tutor should avoid intervention if at all possible and should in any case respect the students' responsibility for the learning.

However, to an inexperienced tutor silence can be highly threatening, and so there is a tendency to intervene too soon if a group appears uncertain what to do. Frustration and anger are also worrying phenomena, and again an inexperienced tutor may intervene too soon to resolve them. But coping with silence, frustration and anger are important skills for the student to acquire, and too early an intervention may pre-empt this learning. Ideally a tutor should withhold his intervention for as long as possible, only interposing if serious disintegration of the group or the exercise seems likely. As said earlier, this skill grows with experience.

Similar skill is needed with the handling of questions. Often students will ask for information which is already contained in the exercise documentation or which they should be able to work out for themselves. Obviously this sort of question should not be answered unless the tutor feels that without the information the exercise will come to an abrupt end. A comment such as 'All the information you need is contained in your briefing sheet' is always preferable, where possible. The reverse of this situation is where students seem incapable of testing the boundaries by asking for information which they need but which they have not been given (as, for example, in *Islands in the Sun*). The tutor will need to develop the skill of knowing how long to hold back before suggesting to the students that they should ask for help.

The review

The most important part of any exercise is the *Review*. It is here that the students will be able to discuss and unravel what they have learnt from the exercise. It is essential that they should have a chance to do this for themselves before there are any comments from the observers or the tutor. The tutor will need the skill to draw this learning out from them rather than attempting to supply them with it. He must try to get the participants to describe their experience rather than describing his own! In this context is it more productive to concentrate on questions rather than statements. 'What were you thinking when you did that?' or 'What were the advantages and disadvantages of your course of action?' are far more likely to produce perceptive responses than statements such as 'The mistake you made was . . .' or 'If you had done it this way . . .' The words What?, Why?, When?, How?, Where?, and Who? can introduce questions which will encourage students to explore the experiences they have been through.

When the observers come to make their comments, they should be encouraged to describe what they have seen and heard rather than to make value judgements about it. They are, as it were, the mirrors into which the students can look to draw their own conclusions as to their performance and behaviour. The temptation to 'score points' over others must be avoided. Observed behaviour is after all only a clue (and nothing more) to the underlying motivation and experience.

Whatever the skills of the tutor or the observers, the most significant part of the *Review* is likely to be the learning which the participants can acquire for themselves. A number of models can help draw this out. Two of the most useful are the *Process Analysis Questionnaire* (see Figure 2 on pages 24–25) and the *Inter-personal Traits Questionnaire* (see Figure 3 on pages 26–27). The former is the easier to use, being less time-consuming and 'safer' in that it is less likely to provoke the expression and exchange of feelings between participants. The latter is particularly useful in generating more open discussion about the behaviour of the participants. It also helps increase skill in giving and receiving feedback.

Evaluation

In exercises involving behaviourally-based learning it is often difficult, if not impossible, to know exactly what learning has taken place. Nevertheless, the tutor will still want to evaluate the activity in order to assess the success (or otherwise) of the exercise and to gauge, as best he can, the learning which has emerged from it. In addition to this personal evaluation, it is often helpful to finish every session or module of work with an opportunity for participants to evaluate what has taken place, what they have contributed to the learning, and their views of the exercise, other inputs and presentation. While this evaluation can easily be conducted as part of the *Review*, it may be better in the long term for students to make written comments. They will then build up a 'diary' to which they can refer in order to trace the experiences through which they have passed and, it is hoped, to monitor their growth in maturity and skill. It may be useful to devise a basic form on which this can be done, as shown in Figure 4 on page 28.

Sensitivity   As will have become apparent, the single most important quality which a tutor needs is sensitivity. This embraces understanding the needs (learning and emotional) of the students; the ability to encourage them to dwell on their experiences, and articulate and analyse their feelings and behaviour; an appreciation of the place of confidentiality in much experiential learning; the instinct which knows when to intervene and when to remain in the background; and the ability to support and counsel participants who, having exposed their feelings, find it difficult to handle them. This may sound a daunting catalogue, but, from the very fact that a tutor is anxious to help in presenting experiential learning, it is likely that the sensitivity is there, at least in embryonic form, and can be developed through training and practice.

Tutor training   Courses which will help tutors acquire the skills needed for development training and for the presentation of experiential learning are available at many university departments, colleges of higher and further education, and other specialist centres. However, there is so much to be gained from the staff of a school or college training and undergoing experiential learning together, that this is strongly recommended. Not only will individuals gain the skills and confidence to introduce this style of learning to their students, but also a common culture will be developed and a strategy for experiential learning in the institution can be devised. If difficulty is encountered in setting up a staff development programme of this kind, help may well be obtained from one of the agencies described in Chapter 1 (page 11) or by consulting the information bank at the Centre for the Study of Comprehensive Schools (CSCS) based at Wentworth College, York University.

How to use the Process analysis questionnaire

1 Against each statement on the questionnaire, place a tick in one of the columns 1–8 according to how strongly you agree or disagree.

2 Compare your scores with those of the others in your group.

3 Identify the areas in which there is a wide divergence (say 4 points or more) between yourself and others or among the others.

4 Discuss these areas of disagreement and try to identify reasons for them. You may also want to look at areas where you all scored either very high or very low.

Figure 2

PROCESS ANALYSIS QUESTIONNAIRE

	STRONGLY DISAGREE							STRONGLY AGREE
	1	2	3	4	5	6	7	8
1 I feel satisfied with the way we planned our work								
2 We all agreed on our aims and methods								
3 We used our time to good effect								
4 We made the best use of our resources								
5 We organised ourselves well								
6 We were lively and imaginative in our approach								
7 The group showed a lot of interest in what we were doing								
8 We were all involved in decision making								
9 The group resolved its disagreements								
10 I felt committed to the group								
11 I listened when others were speaking								
12 The others listened when I was speaking								
13 I was encouraged by the group to make a contribution								
14 I had influence on our decisions								
15 There were ways in which I could have helped the group more								
16 I had information, thoughts or feelings I kept to myself								
17 There were ways in which I hindered the group								
18 I enjoyed working in the group								
19 The group felt comfortable								
20 The group was dominated by some members								

The inter-personal traits questionnaire
(For use with groups of 6 or less)

Individual instructions for use

1 You have been supplied with a questionnaire form for each member of the group in which you are working, including yourself.

2 Fill in a separate questionnaire form for each of the other members of the group and one for yourself.

3 Give each person in the group the questionnaire you have filled in on him or her. In return you will receive a questionnaire from each other member.

4 On the form you have filled in on yourself, insert the summary of scores contained in the questionnaires submitted to you by the other group members (lettered A to E).

5 Identify those areas in which there is a wide divergence of opinion (3 points or more) between yourself and others, or among the others.

6 In the total group, or in smaller groups, discuss these areas of divergence and try to identify reasons for them. You may also want to look at areas where you are generally thought to score particularly high or low.

Figure 3

INTER-PERSONAL TRAITS QUESTIONNAIRE

PERSON RATED ―――――――

RATED BY ―――――

	VERY LOW ―――――→ VERY HIGH									SELF	SUMMARY				
	1	2	3	4	5	6	7	8			A	B	C	D	E
1 Ability to listen in an understanding way															
2 Ability to express feelings openly															
3 Tendency to dominate groups or meetings															
4 Ability to help others think through problems															
5 Ability to accept help from others															
6 Ability to influence others															
7 Tendency towards autocratic approach															
8 Tendency towards consultative approach															
9 Faces up to conflict and hostility															
10 Accepts warmth and affection															
11 Ability to express ideas clearly															
12 Ability to originate new ideas															

Figure 4

EVALUATION SHEET

No: ——

	What did we do?	What did I learn?	What did I contribute?	What were the good points? How could it have been improved?
Date: **Topic/Activity:**				
Date: **Topic/Activity:**				
Date: **Topic/Activity:**				
Date: **Topic/Activity**				

4 Observation techniques

The most important part of any exercise is the *Review*, the chance to examine and learn from the process of the exercise rather than the task. It is essential that this process is adequately recorded so that full learning value can be obtained from it. Participants are not ideally placed to make these observations. They are likely to be so closely involved in the task that they are able to pay only fleeting attention to the process, even if they are experienced. The role of the observer is to mirror and reflect back to the participants what has been happening, and this is vital to the success of an exercise. In an ideal situation one would hope to have experienced trained observers available to fulfil this function. But in a normal school or college setting only one or at best two tutors are likely to be available, so it is important that the participants develop sufficient skill to be able to observe each other and provide the appropriate feed-back. In the long run this may be more valuable than having trained outside observers present, as the skills the participants will need to acquire are all highly relevant to the general learning which a development training programme hopes to transmit. In addition to perceptive observation this includes careful listening, the understanding of non-verbal communication, sensitive giving of feed-back, and the avoidance of inappropriate value judgements.

This chapter aims to provide aids to improving observation skills. These include three specific observation exercises; hints on observation skills both at a simple and a more advanced level; and a *Time Analysis sheet* with instructions for its use. The three exercises are deliberately designed to be confusing and are therefore not normally usable for other purposes. If more observation exercises are needed, some of the more action-centred ones such as *News-stand, Scramble, Furniture Removers* or *Boom! Boom!* are appropriate.

The introduction of observation skills   A session to introduce observation skills can be started by providing each participant with an *Observation skills* sheet (Figure 5 shows a simple sheet, Figure 6 a more advanced version) and taking them through it step by step. The group can be divided into two halves, one half tackling one of the exercises and the other half observing. After the normal *Review*, the roles of the group can be reversed so that every participant gets an opportunity to observe. More experienced observers may wish to use the *Time analysis* sheet (Figure 7 on page 32) which helps participants see exactly which aspects of behaviour predominate in their group work.

Figure 5 **Some simple observation skills**

1 Your aim as an observer is
 • to watch what is going on
 • to listen to what is being said
 • to make helpful comments after the exercise is complete

Do
 • watch and listen carefully
 • remember that you can learn a lot not only from what people say and do, but from their eyes, voices, hands, position in their chair, and so on
 • write down the important things you see and hear (the exact words if possible)
 • move to where you can see and hear best without disturbing those taking part

Do not
 • get involved in the exercise
 • say anything to anyone until the exercise is over

2 If you are a general observer, there are two main things to look for.

a The task
Was the task completed? Successfully?
Was it properly planned?
Was the plan kept to?
Did it get done in time?
b The group
How did the group arrange the chairs? The room?

Did the group choose a leader? How was this done?
Who actually led the group at first? Later?
Did anyone keep a record? Officially or unofficially?
Did anyone keep the time? Officially or unofficially?
Did everyone take part?
Was everyone listened to?
Was anyone ignored?
Was anyone 'being a comedian'?
Was anyone being obstructive?
How were any decisions reached:
 • by careful reasoning?
 • by a vote?
 • by one/a few imposing their views on the rest?

3 If you are asked to observe one particular person, ask yourself the following questions.
Did he/she have a part to play—at first? —later?
Did he/she take the lead at any stage?
Was he/she really interested in completing the task successfully?
Was he/she listened to with respect? If not, why not?
Was he/she ignored? If so, why?
Did he/she share any information he/she had with the others?
Did he/she listen to other people?
Could you tell anything about what he/she felt from his/her eyes? voice? hands? position of the body? anything else?

Figure 6 **More advanced observation skills**

1 *Organisation*
Did the group organise its working environment satisfactorily? Was it workmanlike? comfortable?
Did the group make arrangements to share? to record? to display information?
Was the group conscious of time? How was this achieved?

2 *Leadership*
Did the group have a leader? Did it need one?
How was the leader chosen: appointed? volunteered? some other way?
Did the leader in fact lead? If not, why not?
Who led the group unofficially in its various stages?
Was this leadership helpful or unhelpful?
If there was an official leader, did he/she
- keep the group moving?
- keep to any plans that had been made?
- keep control of the time?
- prevent unnecessary diversion?
- involve everyone present?
- maintain a good atmosphere?
- evaluate contributions as they were made?
- summarise conclusions?

3 *Planning*
Did the group have a plan? Did it need one?
Was sufficient time spent in preparing this plan?
Did the plan cover all foreseeable eventualities?
Did the group adhere to the plan?
If the group abandoned or modified the plan in action, was it right to do so?
If not, what caused this change of plan to occur?

4 *Decision making*
Did the group come to any decision?
Was this decision correct?
Was the decision reached by

- consensus?
- majority vote?
- 'sense of the meeting'?
- a 'steamroller' by a minority?
- edict by the leader or some other individual?
- no identifiable means?
Could the decision have been reached more efficiently?
If so, how?

5 *Individuals*
Did everyone in the group take part in the activity?
Did they need to?
Was anyone clearly uninterested? Was it possible to see why?
Was anyone given unexpected precedence or influence? Why?
Was anyone ignored? Why?
Was anyone snubbed? isolated? Why? Did the group contain a comedian? a cynic? an obstructionist?
Who in the group could be seen as
- an initiator or ideas person?
- a follower?
- a facilitator for the group or for individuals?
- an enquirer?
- an evaluator?

6 *Behaviour*
How would you describe the atmosphere of the group? Who or what gave it this atmosphere?
Did you learn anything about the group or individuals from the body language of those present?
Were there any clear signs of emotion or feeling in the group?
What were they? What caused them?
Did you notice any norms or unwritten rules of behaviour in the group?
If so, what? Why did they exist? Did they help or hinder the work of the group?

Figure 7

TIME ANALYSIS SHEET

	INDIVIDUALS								GROUP		
	Giving facts	Asking for facts	Giving opinions	Asking for opinions	Giving clarification/ summary	Asking for clarification/ summary	Supporting others or elaborating	Clarifying procedures/ suggesting procedures	Disagreeing	Interrupting	Joking or straying	Totals	Several talking	Silence
A														
B														
C														
D														
E														
F														
G														
H														
Totals														

How to use the time analysis sheet

1 Use the list of *Definitions* to familiarise yourself with the type of contribution to be recorded in each column of the sheet.

2 Identify each member of the group with one of the letters **A** to **H**.

3 For periods of 5 minutes at a time, record on the sheet the contribution of each member of the group. If several members are talking at the same time, or if there is silence, record this in the appropriate column under 'Group'.

4 Continue this process at intervals of 5 minutes – ie 5 minutes record, 5 minutes rest . . .

5 When the exercise ends, transfer the data you have collected on to a summary sheet without disclosing which member of the group corresponds to which letter. If possible this summary sheet should be large enough to be seen by all.

6 Ask members of the group to look at the summary sheet and identify which letter they each are. Encourage the group to help those who find this difficult. (There is generally much humour and little threat in this process.)

7 Discuss the implications of what has emerged. Who needs to listen more or be encouraged more? Does the group plan its procedures and aims properly? . . .

Time analysis

Some definitions

Giving facts *Asking for facts*	These refer to genuine attempts to further discussion on the basis of provable fact eg 'All those words begin with the letter G'. They contrast with giving or asking for opinions.
Giving opinions *Asking for opinions*	Statements which are non-factual eg 'My feeling is that . . .', 'What do you think, Sue?', 'This exercise is a waste of time' . . .
Giving clarification/ *summary* *Asking for clarification/* *summary*	Any statement which seeks to clarify or summarise what has happened to date, eg 'What we have decided so far is then . . .', 'What do you mean by . . .?'

Supporting others *Elaborating*	Any contribution which gives backing to or adds to another's statement, eg 'That's absolutely right', 'What is more, we can also . . .'.
Clarifying/suggesting *procedures/aims*	Attempts to establish or remind the group about the way it should be operating, eg 'I thought Bill was recording this'.
Disagreeing	Statements which indicate opposition to another point of view, eg 'I can't go along with that'.
Interrupting	Any example of a member of the group cutting across what another member is saying or across a conversation already taking place.

LITTLE BOXES

Objective

- to develop observation skills

Description

The group is asked to sort a jumbled variety of paper clips and safety pins into matchboxes. They are not given sufficient data or any criteria by which to structure the solution of the task. This is likely to produce difficulty, frustration and possibly confusion, all of which will provide opportunities for the observers to improve their skill

Target group

Years 1–3

Organisation

One or two groups of 5; remainder act as observers
One tutor per group if possible

Time required

45 minutes (minimum)

Tutor skill

B (see page 17)

Location

Any suitable room. If two groups take part, two rooms are better

Materials

10 or 12 empty matchboxes of different sizes. An envelope containing as many paper clips and safety pins of different sizes, types and colours as you can afford

Tutor's notes

1. Brief the whole class on observation skills (see p 30) (*10 minutes*)

2. Divide the class in half. From each half choose a working group and an observing group.

3. If two rooms are not available, get the working groups to sit in two circles as far apart as possible. Place the matchboxes and the envelope containing paper clips and safety pins on the floor in the middle. (*5 minutes*)

4. Read out the following:

    The envelope contains paper clips, safety pins and matchboxes. The task of your group is to put the clips and pins into the boxes as you think appropriate. You have 15 minutes for this task. You will be timed from the moment any member of the group touches the envelope. I can give you no further information.

    (*15 minutes minimum*)

5. *Review*, based on observers' findings and the original briefing on observation skills (*15 minutes*)

RANKING 1/RANKING 2

Objective

- to develop observation skills

Description

In *Ranking 1* the group is asked to place a number of 'service' occupations in rank order, without being given any criteria for doing so. This is likely to produce difficulty, frustration and possibly confusion, all of which will provide opportunity for the observers to improve their skill. There should also be some learning about consensus and influencing skills.
Ranking 2 is similar to *Ranking 1*, but uses occupations taken from the broader school setting.

Target group

Ranking 1 Years 3–5
Ranking 2 6th form and staff

Organisation

One group of 10; remainder act as observers
One tutor

Time required

1 hour (minimum)

Tutor skill

B (see page 17)

Location

Any suitable room

Materials

One briefing sheet per participant

Tutor's notes

1. Brief the whole class on observation skills (see p 30) (*10 minutes*)

2. Get the working group to arrange the room as they want it. Issue briefing sheets and invite the group to start work. (In some cases the group may need reminding that they are to produce a *group* solution, otherwise they will give up too easily.) (*25 minutes*)

3. *Review* based on observers' findings and the original briefing on observation skills (*25 minutes minimum*)

LEARNING
IN *ACTION*

The task of your group is to place the following in order from 1 to 10

Clergyman	Member of Parliament
Doctor	Milkman
Dustman	Newsagent
Garage mechanic	Police officer
Headteacher	Postal worker

You have 25 minutes in which to complete this task

LEARNING
IN *ACTION*

The task of your group is to place the following in order from 1 to 12

Area adviser	Form tutor
Caretaker	Groundsman
Catering superintendent	Head boy/girl
Chairman of governors	Headteacher
Chairman of PTA	Maintenance officer
County Education Officer	School Secretary

You have 25 minutes in which to complete this task

PART 2

The Exercises

BOOM! BOOM!

Objectives	• to improve planning skills and time control • to improve observation skills
Description	Two tasks are superimposed—counting the occurrence of particular letters in a piece of text and marking the passage of time by specific 'calls'. The groups undertake these tasks in competition with each other. The conflicting pressures will produce a degree of chaos and hence a medium for exploring behaviour.
Target group	Years 3–5, 6th form, staff (For less academically-able pupils the exercise can be simplified by omitting some combination of 'Bip', 'Bap' and 'Bop'.)
Organisation	Groups of 4 One/two tutors for the exercise plus one observer per participant
Time required	35–45 minutes
Tutor skill	A (see page 17)
Location	Room large enough for all groups to work in
Materials	One briefing sheet per group One copy of *Directions to Nethermill School* per group One *Bip, Bap, Bop* sheet per observer A large clock with second hand

Tutor's notes

1. Check that there is a wall clock or equivalent with second hand in the room.

2. Issue a briefing sheet to each group. Attach an observer (equipped with *Bip, Bap, Bop* sheet) to each participant. While groups are studying briefing sheets and preparing plans, brief observers. Each observer must know exactly what his subject's part is in the group plan, so that he can monitor that person's actions, especially his calls. Explain that things are going to happen very fast. (*10 minutes*)

3. Issue each group with a copy of *Directions to Nethermill School*. Groups work on the exercise, finishing when the first group claims to have calculated the letters. The correct solution is:

   A – 47
   E – 45
   I – 34
   O – 64
   U – 19

   If the answer given is incorrect, carry on until a correct solution is found. (*5 minutes?*)

4. Check scores, announce winner. (*5 minutes*)

5. *Review*
   a *The plan*
   - did participants realise that it is not possible for any person to undertake both tasks simultaneously?
   b *The group*
   - did participants keep calm if things started to go wrong?
   c *The parallels*
   - how are routine and one-off commitments integrated into the same programme?
   (*15 minutes minimum*)

1 You are about to take part in a competition against the other group(s). The competition will begin in 10 minutes time when you will be issued with an A4 sheet of typescript. It will end when a team finds the correct solution. The first team to finish will receive 50 points.

2 Each team starts with 100 points. The winning team is the one with most points when the competition ends.

3 Use the next 10 minutes to plan your action and arrange your working space.

4 Your task will be –

  a to calculate the number of times the following letters appear in the typescript: *a, e, i, o, u,*

  b to make the following calls:
- every 13 seconds   –   BIP
- every 21 seconds   –   BAP
- every 32 seconds   –   BOP
- every minute   –   BOOM! BOOM!

  The calls must be loud enough to be heard by your observer(s).

5 For every missed, incorrect or wrongly-timed call your team forfeits 10 points.

Minutes	Seconds		Minutes	Seconds	
0	13	BIP	5	12	BIP
0	21	BAP	5	15	BAP
0	26	BIP	5	20	BOP
0	32	BOP	5	25	BIP
0	39	BIP	5	36	BAP
0	42	BAP	5	38	BIP
0	52	BIP	5	51	BIP
1	00	BOOM! BOOM!	5	52	BOP
1	03	BAP	5	57	BAP
1	04	BOP	6	00	BOOM! BOOM!
1	05	BIP	6	04	BIP
1	18	BIP	6	17	BIP
1	24	BAP	6	18	BAP
1	31	BIP	6	24	BOP
1	36	BOP	6	30	BIP
1	44	BIP	6	39	BAP
1	45	BAP	6	43	BIP
1	57	BIP	6	56	BIP/BOP
2	00	BOOM! BOOM!	7	00	BOOM! BOOM!/BOP
2	06	BAP	7	09	BIP
2	08	BOP	7	21	BAP
2	10	BIP	7	22	BIP
2	23	BIP	7	28	BOP
2	27	BAP	7	35	BIP
2	36	BIP	7	42	BAP
2	40	BOP	7	48	BIP
2	48	BAP	8	00	BOOM! BOOM!/BOP
2	49	BIP	8	01	BIP
3	00	BOOM! BOOM!	8	03	BAP
3	02	BIP	8	14	BIP
3	09	BAP	8	24	BAP
3	12	BOP	8	27	BIP
3	15	BIP	8	32	BOP
3	28	BIP	8	40	BIP
3	30	BAP	8	45	BAP
3	41	BIP	8	53	BIP
3	44	BOP	9	00	BOOM! BOOM!
3	51	BAP	9	04	BOP
3	54	BIP	9	06	BIP/BAP
4	00	BOOM! BOOM!	9	19	BIP
4	07	BIP	9	27	BAP
4	12	BAP	9	32	BIP
4	16	BOP	9	36	BOP
4	20	BIP	9	45	BIP
4	33	BIP/BAP	9	48	BAP
4	46	BIP	9	58	BIP
4	48	BOP	10	00	BOOM! BOOM!
4	54	BAP			
4	59	BIP			
5	00	BOOM! BOOM!			

© 1987   Roger Kirk   Basil Blackwell

BOOM! BOOM!
Directions to Nethermill School, Denbigh

Come down motorway, leaving motorway by exit 16 onto A543. Travel along A543 until you come to a roundabout, go right around and turn off onto road marked Denbigh. Continue along road passing a school on the right hand side, then take right turn at the end of the school building. Go right down to bottom of this road (two landmarks at the bottom are BBC Building and a Launderette) and turn right onto Nethermill Lane. Travel along and take 2nd turn right which leads onto Overmill Avenue. Go almost to the top and take only left turn. Travel a few hundred yards and the school is on the right. Go right around the school building to the car park which is at the front of the building.

CLASSROOM CORRIDOR

Objective	• to examine behaviour and organisation within a group
Description	The group is required to tackle a logical problem which would be easier to solve on an individual basis. Only one copy of the essential data is provided so normal individual processes are discouraged. This could be called 'an exercise in confusion', and is likely to lead to frustration and a degree of chaos
Target group	Above-average pupils from years 4 and 5; 6th form and staff
Organisation	Groups of 5–6
	One/two tutors plus observers
Time required	1 hour (minimum)
Tutor skills	B (see page 17)
Location	Any room in which groups can work with reasonable privacy
Materials	One copy of the *Classroom Corridor* briefing sheet per person or (to make the exercise more complex) one or two per group

Tutor's notes

1. Issue briefing sheets. The number can vary from one per person to one per group, depending on age, ability, experience and available time. The fewer the sheets issued, the longer the exercise will take.

2. Invite groups to work on the exercise. (*30 minutes or until complete*)

3. Discuss logic of the solution. (*5 minutes*)

4. *Review*
   Groups should be encouraged to consider:
   • organisation of the group—roles; leadership; do all need to take part?
   • sharing and display of essential information (especially when only one copy of the briefing sheet is available)
   • any relevant interpersonal behaviour (*25 minutes*)

5. *Solution*

Room	Name	Age	Subject	Instrument
1	Chalk	24	French	Flute
2	Tough	39	Maths	Percussion
3	Brain	43	English	Harp
4	Penn	27	Physics	Violin
5	Cribb	51	Art	Tuba

   Mrs Brain is 43
   The Maths teacher plays percussion

One logical approach to finding the solution might be as follows.

1. Fill in instant data supplied (4, 7, 9, 11)

R	N	A	S	I
1				Flute
2	Tough			
3				
4	Penn			
5			Art	

2. Miss Cribb must be in Room 3 or Room 5 (1).

   As Miss Chalk is the youngest (5), and the occupant of Room 3 is older than the occupant of Room 2 (12), she must be in Room 1 or Room 5. Mrs Brain teaches English (14), and therefore cannot be in Room 5 but must be in Room 1 or Room 3. But as she plays the harp (2) and the teacher in Room 1 plays the flute (9), she must be in Room 3.

   This means that Miss Chalk can only be in Room 1 and Miss Cribb in Room 5

R	N	A	S	I
1	Chalk			Flute
2	Tough			
3	Brain			
4	Penn			
5	Cribb		Art	

3. Other data can now be filled in

R	N	A	S	I
1	Chalk	24	French	Flute
2	Tough			
3	Brain		English	Harp
4	Penn			
5	Cribb		Art	

4. The violinist and the percussionist are in Rooms 2 and 4 (13), but which way round is not yet clear. However, this means the tuba player must be in Room 5 and the oldest teacher (3).

   As the Maths teacher is not next to the oldest teacher (10), she must be in Room 2 and the Physics teacher in Room 4.

   As the violinist does not teach Maths (6), he must therefore teach Physics, so the Maths teacher is the percussionist.

   As the Physics teacher is 27 (15), and the occupant of Room 3 is older then the occupant of Room 2 (12), Mrs Brain must be 43 and Mrs Tough 39.

Mrs Brain, Miss Chalk, Miss Cribb, Mr Penn and Mrs Tough teach in the Classroom Corridor in five rooms numbered consecutively from Room 1 to Room 5. They are all different ages (51, 43, 39, 27, 24) and they all teach different subjects (Art, English, French, Maths, Physics). By coincidence, they all play different instruments in the School Orchestra (flute, harp, percussion, tuba, violin).

The following facts are known:

1 Mr Penn and Miss Cribb have rooms next to each other.

2 The English teacher plays the harp.

3 The oldest teacher plays the tuba.

4 Mrs Tough teaches in Room 2.

5 Miss Chalk is the youngest teacher.

6 The violinist does not teach Maths.

7 The Art teacher is in Room 5.

8 The French teacher is not next to the English teacher.

9 The flute player is in Room 1.

10 The Maths teacher is not next to the oldest teacher.

11 The Art teacher is next to Mr Penn.

12 The teacher in Room 3 is older than the teacher in Room 2.

13 There is one room between the violinist and the percussionist.

14 Mrs Brain teaches English.

15 The Physics teacher is 27 years old.

How old is Mrs Brain?
What instrument does the Maths teacher play?

NEWS-STAND

Objective
- to develop skills in joint problem solving, planning and group development

Description
The group is asked to plan and carry out the re-assembling of a box of 'scrambled' newspapers. At the planning stage they are given no information other than a statement of the task itself.

Target group
Pupils (all ages and abilities) and staff

Organisation
Groups of 5–6

One/two tutors plus observers

Time required
45 minutes

Tutor skill
C (see page 17)

Location
Any room large enough to give the groups adequate working space. With newspapers to sort out, this space may be larger than you imagine. There is no need for group privacy

Materials
One large, sealed, cardboard box per group containing 5–10 newspapers broken down into single sheets and mixed up.

When selecting newspapers, the following points need to be remembered:

a key factors which will arise in the groups' planning of the task are title, date, size, shape, colour, type of paper

b the more papers there are, the harder the exercise becomes

c the difficulty can be varied by the way in which the newspapers are placed in the box eg separate sheets; sheets folded back to front; sheets upside down; 'false' newspapers made up of pages from different dates

Tutor's notes

1. Decide on the composition of the newspapers. Break them down, mix up the sheets and place them in sealed boxes.

2. Divide the class into groups of 5–6.

3. Read out the following:

   This box contains sheets of newspaper. The task of your group is to reassemble these sheets. The newspapers must not be damaged. You have up to 15 minutes in which to plan this task. It must then be completed as quickly as possible. You will be timed for the task from the moment any member of the group touches the box. I can give you no further information.

4. *Review*
   Points that should emerge will include:
   - how did the group define 'reassemble'?
   - was the group successful in completing the task?
   - did the group have a plan?
   - did they stick to their plan?
   - how did the leadership of the group develop?
   - did every member of the group have a role?

- how was the working area arranged physically?
- did the group keep a proper check on time?
- did the group compete with other groups?
- did any group try to find out what other groups were doing?
- any relevant inter-personal behaviour.

(*20 minutes*)

FURNITURE REMOVERS

Objective   • to practise the planning and organising of group activities

Description   Participants are required to plan and carry out the task of removing and
                      replacing a quantity of furniture. If planning has not been sufficiently
                      detailed, chaos will result

Target group   Years 1–5 (all abilities)

Organisation   The class works as one group
                      One tutor (observers optional)

Time required   45 minutes

Tutor skill   C (see page 17)

Location   Any normal classroom or class working area, but the exercise will work
                      better if:

                      a it is not immediately adjacent to other rooms because of possible noise
                      b it is a ground-floor room with more than one exit (eg a fire-door, or large
                      window)
                      c the furniture in it is not particularly new or good—in case of accidents

Materials   None

Tutor's notes

1. Ask the group to choose a leader, or appoint one yourself.

2. With younger pupils it may be more successful to brief the leader and the
   group members together. Otherwise, brief the leader as follows:

   All the members of the group are working on this task together. Divide
   the group into two halves. The job of the first half is to remove all the
   tables (chairs, desks. . .) from the room as quickly and as quietly as
   possible. The job of the second half is to return them to the exact
   positions they were in originally. You have up to 20 minutes in which to
   plan this operation, and 5 minutes in which to carry it out.
   (The time can be varied according to the age and ability of the pupils, the
   size of the room and the kind of furniture involved.)

3. Groups work on the activity. (*25 minutes*)

4. *Review*
   Points which should emerge will include:

   • was the task achieved to time?

   • how successful was the leader?

   • was there a proper plan? If so, was it workable—use of all possible
   exits, methods of identifying original position of furniture. . ?

   • how was the group organised?

   • did everyone work together or were the two halves competing with
   each other?

   • was it carried out quickly and quietly?

(*20 minutes*)

EVENING OUT

Objectives
- to help in the planning of priorities
- to improve negotiating and influencing skills

Description
Members of the group are asked to plan their engagements (school, domestic and leisure) for a typical week. They are then required to resolve, by mutual persuasion, conflicts which may arise between them.

Target group
Years 3–5

Organisation
Groups of 5
One/two tutors plus observers

Time required
1 hour (minimum) plus preliminary work

Tutor skill
C (see page 17)

Location
Any room in which groups can work with reasonable privacy

Materials
One briefing sheet per participant (these are in sets of five, all different—each group member should have a different sheet).
One timetable form per participant.

Tutor's notes

1. *Stage 1* Issue briefing sheets and timetables. Ask pupils to complete task 1 individually. (This could well be a task for homework or private study.)

2. *Stage 2* Divide the class into groups of 5. Invite groups to work on task 2. (*25 minutes*)

3. *Stage 3* Get pupils to examine each others' timetables and check which groups were most successful at doing activities together and which individuals were most persuasive. (*10 minutes*)

4. *Review*
   There are two main themes: priorities and influencing. Points which should emerge will include:

   a Priorities
   - how many of the activities were pupils able to get into their timetables?
   - what did they discard and on what grounds?
   - did they try any negotiating with parents where necessary?
   - were they flexible—*average* time of homework, possible use of week-ends etc?
   - how did they use the timetable forms?

   b Influencing
   - who was most successful at influencing? How? Why?
   - did pupils help each other in planning their respective timetables?
   - did they share relevant information? How?

   (*25 minutes*)

You and your special group of friends enjoy doing most things together. Next week is a typical one. On Monday you would all like to go to the Youth Club from 7.30–10.30. On Tuesday there is a school trip to the Sports Centre for ice skating. This leaves school at 6.30 and returns by 9.30. On Wednesday you always like to meet up at one of your houses to play your tapes and discs. On Thursday you all generally go to the High Street Coffee Bar anytime from 6.30 onwards where you meet up with other friends. On Friday there is a disco at the Purple Cellar Club. This lasts from 8–11.30 and is extremely popular.

Your evenings are generally fairly flexible as tea (which lasts about half an hour) can be at any time, and your parents are not worried what time you go to bed. However, when you get back from school at 4.00, you have a paper round to carry out (1 hour), and the dog needs a walk every evening (30 minutes). On Monday, Wednesday and Thursday you get 1 hour's homework, and twice a week you have to muck out the rabbits (1 hour). In addition, on either Monday or Tuesday evening your Dad expects a couple of hours help from you in his workshop.

Your task is:

1 To work out, on the form provided, your evening timetable for next week.

2 To persuade your group of friends to come to your home on Wednesday to play tapes and discs.

LEARNING
IN *ACTION*

You and your special group of friends enjoy doing most things together. Next week is a typical one. On Monday you would all like to go to the Youth Club from 7.30–10.30. On Tuesday there is a school trip to the Sports Centre for ice skating. This leaves school at 6.30 and returns by 9.30. On Wednesday you always like to meet up at one of your houses to play your tapes and discs. On Thursday you all generally go to the High Street Coffee Bar anytime from 6.30 onwards where you meet up with other friends. On Friday there is a disco at the Purple Cellar Club. This lasts from 8–11.30 and is extremely popular.

You get back from school at 4.30 in time for your paper round (1 hour). Tea is at 6, and lasts about half an hour, and your Mum expects you to spend a further half hour every evening tidying and cleaning your room. You are quite keen on your school work, and aim to do 1½ hours homework every night on average, some nights doing more, some less. On either Thursday or Friday evening you spend a couple of hours baby-sitting for your sister. Your bedtime is 10.30 except on Fridays when it is 11.

Your task is:

1 To work out, on the form provided, your evening timetable for next week.

2 To persuade your group of friends to come to the ice-skating on Tuesday.

You and your special group of friends enjoy doing most things together. Next week is a typical one. On Monday you would all like to go to the Youth Club from 7.30–10.30. On Tuesday there is a school trip to the Sports Centre for ice skating. This leaves school at 6.30 and returns by 9.30. On Wednesday you always like to meet up at one of your houses to play your tapes and discs. On Thursday you all generally go to the High Street Coffee Bar anytime from 6.30 onwards where you meet up with other friends. On Friday there is a disco at the Purple Cellar Club. This lasts from 8–11.30 and is extremely popular.

You get back from school at 4 o'clock each day and then spend an hour preparing tea for the family. Tea at 5.30 lasts about half an hour, and you like to set aside half an hour also for a bath, and a further half hour for cleaning and tidying your room. You are extremely concerned about your GCSE courses, always expecting to do 2 hours homework a night. Both the Scouts and the Guides meet for 2 hours every Tuesday and Wednesday evening, and you always try to get to at least one of these meetings. Your parents insist normally on a 10.00 pm bedtime though this is extended to 10.30 on Fridays and on one other day of your choice during the week.

Your task is:

1 To work out, on the form provided, your evening timetable for next week.

2 To persuade your group of friends to come to the disco at the Purple Cellar Club on Friday.

You and your special group of friends enjoy doing most things together. Next week is a typical one. On Monday you would all like to go to the Youth Club from 7.30–10.30. On Tuesday there is a school trip to the Sports Centre for ice skating. This leaves school at 6.30 and returns by 9.30. On Wednesday you always like to meet up at one of your houses to play your tapes and discs. On Thursday you all generally go to the High Street Coffee Bar anytime from 6.30 onwards where you meet up with other friends. On Friday there is a disco at the Purple Cellar Club. This lasts from 8–11.30 and is extremely popular.

You get back from school at 4 pm and then you always go round to your Grandma for an hour to help her with any jobs or chores that need doing. Tea is at 6.00, and you have to allow an hour for this as you help with clearing away and washing up afterwards. However, on either Friday or Monday (you can decide which you prefer) you help out at your Uncle's corner shop between 5 and 7, and tea is then at 7. With exams getting closer you allow two hours for homework every night. Bedtime is 10.30, and your parents are strict about this, though you can occasionally get an extension.

Your task is:

1 To work out, on the form provided, your evening timetable for next week.

2 To persuade your group of friends all to come to the High Street Coffee Bar on Thursday for as long as possible.

You and your special group of friends enjoy doing most things together. Next week is a typical one. On Monday you would all like to go to the Youth Club from 7.30–10.30. On Tuesday there is a school trip to the Sports Centre for ice skating. This leaves school at 6.30 and returns by 9.30. On Wednesday you always like to meet up at one of your houses to play your tapes and discs. On Thursday you all generally go to the High Street Coffee Bar anytime from 6.30 onwards where you meet up with other friends. On Friday there is a disco at the Purple Cellar Club. This lasts from 8–11.30 and is extremely popular.

Organising your evenings is quite easy for you as tea (lasting half an hour) can be at any time and you can go to bed when you like. Your parents get annoyed, however, if you go to bed later than 10.30 too often. You get home from school at 4.30, and your only regular commitments are taking the dog for a walk (30 minutes) and an average of half an hour's homework nightly. The ferrets need mucking out twice a week, but that only takes an hour a time. However, your Dad expects you on either Wednesday or Thursday to help him in his fish and chip van from 7 to 10 pm.

Your task is:

1 To work out, on the form provided, your evening timetable for next week.

2 To persuade your group of friends to come to the Youth Club on Monday.

	MONDAY	TUESDAY	WEDNESDAY	THURSDAY	FRIDAY
4.00					
4.30					
5.00					
5.30					
6.00					
6.30					
7.00					
7.30					
8.00					
8.30					
9.00					
9.30					
10.00					
10.30					

FIRST THINGS FIRST

Objective	• to help in the planning of priorities
Description	A practical exercise for the least academically-able, to help them plan their time and establish priorities
Target group	Years 1–3 with learning difficulties
Organisation	*Stage 1*: individual *Stage 2*: groups of 4–5 *Stage 3*: plenary One/two tutors
Time required	1¼ hours
Tutor skill	B (see page 17)
Location	Plenary room and group working areas which give reasonable privacy
Materials	One board and set of cards per pupil (These will need to be made in advance. Master cards and blanks are provided, these should be photocopied—preferably on to thin card—and cut out.)

Tutor's notes

1. Distribute a board and a set of cards to each pupil. Extra relevant cards may be added or substitutes made. (*5 minutes*)

2. Ask pupils to work out on the board their evening time-table for the week. (Tutors will have to use their discretion as to how many of the inevitable questions they answer. This will probably depend on the ability of the group.) (*20 minutes*)

3. Form pupils into groups of 4–5. Get them to compare their different solutions and try to produce a common one (*25 minutes*)

4. *Review*
   Points which should emerge will include:
   • how did pupils establish their priorities? What was discussed?
   • testing boundaries: did pupils try to negotiate a new bed-time? move items to the week-end? double-up items such as homework and record-player?
   • any relevant group behaviour.
   (*20–30 minutes*)

c

FIRST THINGS FIRST
Board

LEARNING IN *ACTION*

	MONDAY	TUESDAY	WEDNESDAY	THURSDAY	FRIDAY
4.30					
5.00					
5.30					
6.00					
6.30					
7.00					
7.30					
8.00					
8.30					
9.00					
9.30					
10.00					
BED					

© 1987   Roger Kirk   Basil Blackwell

TEA ½ HOUR	WALK DOG ½ HOUR	WASH UP ½ HOUR	BATH ½ HOUR	PAPER ROUND
TEA ½ HOUR	WALK DOG ½ HOUR	WASH UP ½ HOUR	BATH ½ HOUR	1 HOUR
TEA ½ HOUR	WALK DOG ½ HOUR	WASH UP ½ HOUR	BATH ½ HOUR	PAPER ROUND
TEA ½ HOUR	WALK DOG ½ HOUR	MUCK OUT RABBITS ½ HOUR	TIDY ROOM ½ HOUR	1 HOUR
TEA ½ HOUR	WALK DOG ½ HOUR	MUCK OUT RABBITS ½ HOUR	TIDY ROOM ½ HOUR	PAPER ROUND
TV THURSDAY 'TOP OF THE POPS' 7.00–7.30	TV MONDAY 'CORONATION STREET' 7.30–8.00	TALK TO PARENTS ½ HOUR	TALK TO PARENTS ½ HOUR	1 HOUR
		TALK TO PARENTS ½ HOUR	TALK TO PARENTS ½ HOUR	PAPER ROUND
				1 HOUR
				PAPER ROUND
				1 HOUR

HOMEWORK 1 HOUR	RECORD PLAYER 1 HOUR	MONDAY YOUTH CLUB 7.30–9.30	VISIT GRANDMA 1½ HOURS	FRIDAY BABY SITTING 7.30–10.30
HOMEWORK 1 HOUR	RECORD PLAYER 1 HOUR			
HOMEWORK 1 HOUR	RECORD PLAYER 1 HOUR	THURSDAY DISCO 8.00–10.00	COFFEE BAR 1½ HOURS	
HOMEWORK 1 HOUR	RECORD PLAYER 1 HOUR			
HOMEWORK 1 HOUR	RECORD PLAYER 1 HOUR	WEDNESDAY ICE-SKATING 6.30–8.30		
TV FRIDAY 'BERGERAC' 9.30–10.30	TV WEDNESDAY 'MINDER' 9.00–10.00			

SCRAMBLE

Objectives	• to help establish priorities in planning
	• to examine and improve the working of groups
Description	The groups in competition are asked to plan and carry out the task of cutting out individual letters from a newspaper and placing them in envelopes. The fiddly nature of this activity demands a high degree of planning and organisation.
Target group	Pupils (all ages and abilities) and staff
Organisation	Groups of 4 (or 5)—all groups must be the same size
	One/two tutors plus observers
Time required	1 hour (maximum)
Tutor skill	B (see page 17)
Location	Any room large enough for all the groups (a competitive atmosphere helps, provided each group has sufficient room in which to work)
Materials	One briefing sheet per participant or per group
	Per group:
	One double sheet of a quality newspaper
	26 (old) envelopes
	2 pairs scissors

Tutor's notes

1. Divide participants into groups of 4 and give all participants a briefing sheet. Allow 15 minutes for planning. (*20 minutes*)
2. Issue each group with its equipment. As far as possible newspaper sheets should include a variety of type, and each group should have scissors roughly equivalent in size and quality. (*5 minutes*)
3. Group work. (*5 minutes*)
4. Calculate scores. (*5 minutes*)
5. *Review*
   Points which should emerge will include:
   a Priorities
   • did the groups go for high-scoring letters?—common letters?—random letters?
   b Organisation
   • how did the groups arrange their working areas?
   • how did they divide up the newspaper?
   • how did they allocate the tasks?
   c Planning
   • at what stage did they realise that putting the letters into envelopes was the key factor, rather than cutting out?
   • did this cause them to alter their plans? If so, was the alteration achieved effectively?
   • did they test the boundaries by obtaining extra equipment, trying out who was the most effective cutter etc?

d Dynamics
- the effects of competition
- possible frustrations because of the fiddly nature of the tasks

(*25 minutes*)

SCRAMBLE
Briefing sheet

In 15 minutes time you will be given a double sheet of a quality newspaper, two pairs of scissors and 26 envelopes. Your task will be to cut out as many individual letters as possible from the newspaper and to place them in envelopes. There is one envelope for each letter of the alphabet; all As should be placed in the same envelope, Bs in another and so on.

Your aim is to score the highest possible number of points in 5 minutes. You score points for each letter you cut out and place in an envelope, and there are bonuses available for large numbers of any one letter. The letter values are given below.

Letter values

A	3	J	9	S	4
B	7	K	8	T	2
C	6	L	5	U	6
D	5	M	6	V	8
E	1	N	3	W	6
F	6	O	3	X	9
G	7	P	7	Y	7
H	4	Q	9	Z	9
I	4	R	4		

Bonuses

For every ten letters of one kind in one envelope—10 points
For every twenty letters of one kind in one envelope—20 points
and so on up to a maximum of any one kind of letter: 100 letters—100 points

SURVIVORS

Objectives	• to explore the importance of planning and priorities
	• to improve negotiating skills
Description	Participants are given details of individuals who have survived an air disaster and who are stranded on a remote island. They must plan their response to immediate needs in the light of the situation and the resources available
Target group	*Method A*: years 1–2 (plus older pupils with learning difficulties)
	Method B: years 3–5
	Method C: 6th form
Organisation	Groups of 5
	One/two tutors plus observers
Time required	1 hour
Tutor skill	*Method A* C (see page 17)
	Method B and C B (see page 17)
Location	Any room in which groups can work with reasonable privacy
Materials	One briefing sheet per participant
	(Sheets are in sets of five, all different)

Tutor's notes

1. Distribute briefing sheets to each member of the group.
   Give groups their instructions:

   Method A 'As a group, make a list of all the courses of action you could or should take. Arrange these in an order of priority and allocate tasks to individual survivors.'

   Method B 'What do you do now?'

   Method C No further comments or instructions

2. Groups work on the exercise. (*40 minutes*)

3. *Review*

   Emphasise that there is no 'correct' answer to this problem. Essentially the group has to make a decision as to the relative priorities of survival and escape and work from there.

   However, you may wish to ask the group to discuss:

   • whether they identified the different concerns of the different survivors

   • if they assigned priorities to these concerns

   • how they identified within the group the ability to tackle these concerns

   • if they discussed the practicalities of tackling them

   • whether they noted the possible variables in such matters as the number of concerns that could be tackled simultaneously; the number of survivors required for each job. . .

   • whether they were being realistic

   (*20 minutes*)

LEARNING IN *ACTION*

You are a passenger on flight RKA 072 from Tokyo to Sydney. As the result of a sudden and inexplicable mechanical failure your plane has been forced to ditch in the Pacific Ocean some 400 miles NE of Queensland. You are one of only five survivors who have managed to scramble ashore on a remote, uninhabited and, at first sight, apparently barren island. Apart from the clothes you are wearing, the only possessions you have managed to rescue are your snorkelling equipment and harpoon gun which had been in your cabin luggage.

As a research geographer and climatologist your immediate concern is the heat. You are aware that the midday temperature will be in the region of 35°C, with high humidity. You will be unable to survive for long unless shelter can be provided. From a nearby hill it is possible to get a good view over the island; you can see what appear to be bushes three miles (by your estimate) away to the south, and large outcrops of rock rather further away to the south-west.

SURVIVORS
Survivor 2

LEARNING IN *ACTION*

You are a passenger on flight RKA 072 from Tokyo to Sydney. As the result of a sudden and inexplicable mechanical failure your plane has been forced to ditch in the Pacific Ocean some 400 miles NE of Queensland. The time is 0630 hours. You are one of only five survivors who have managed to scramble ashore on a remote, uninhabited and, at first sight, apparently barren island. Apart from the clothes you are wearing, the only other possession you have managed to rescue is the pair of binoculars you use for bird-watching.

Although you have never imagined yourself being in a situation of this nature, you suppose that your skills as a joiner may be useful in some way. You have a wealth of experience in devising simple wooden structures (garden sheds, pigeon lofts and the like), and have even in the past made a small boat. However, your immediate concern is that you have badly gashed your leg on a rock in scrambling ashore. You have lost a lot of blood and are feeling faint.

SURVIVORS
Survivor 3

LEARNING IN *ACTION*

You are a member of the crew of an Airbus A300 on flight RKA 072 from Tokyo to Sydney. As the result of a sudden and inexplicable mechanical failure, the plane has been forced to ditch in the Pacific Ocean some 400 miles NE of Queensland. You are one of only five survivors who have managed to scramble ashore on a remote, uninhabited and, at first sight, apparently barren island. Apart from your uniform, the only item you managed to bring with you from the plane is a radio transmitter, but you are aware that this is no longer working.

Your professional training and expertise have helped you realise that the plane's disappearance will have been recorded by radar, and that the rescue services will know with some degree of accuracy the area in which your plane has come down. An air and sea search will quickly be mounted, but in an area of this sort it could be days before you are found. You consider it most important to help those involved in the search locate the island where you are stranded.

© 1987   Roger Kirk   Basil Blackwell

SURVIVORS
Survivor 4

LEARNING
IN *ACTION*

You are a State Registered Nurse travelling on flight RKA 072 from Tokyo to Sydney, where you are about to take up a new appointment. As the result of a sudden and inexplicable mechanical failure, your plane has been forced to ditch in the Pacific Ocean some 400 miles NE of Queensland. You are one of only five survivors who have managed to scramble ashore on a remote, uninhabited, and, at first sight, apparently barren island. Apart from the clothes you are wearing, the only other possession you have managed to rescue is your travelling bag of first-aid equipment, which you had with you as cabin luggage.

Given the tropical nature of the island on which you are stranded, your medical training has underlined for you the urgency of finding quickly a supply of drinking water. Without this, survival for more than a day or two will be impossible. Subsequently the need for food will also be important.

SURVIVORS
Survivor 5

LEARNING
IN *ACTION*

You are a passenger on flight RKA 072 from Tokyo to Sydney. As the result of a sudden and inexplicable mechanical failure, the plane has been forced to ditch in the Pacific Ocean some 400 miles NE of Queensland. You are one of only five survivors who have managed to scramble ashore on a remote, uninhabited and, at first sight, apparently barren island. Apart from the clothes you are wearing, you have been able to rescue nothing from the plane.

As a teacher of electronics, you feel that your skills should be of some use, but you are not sure what. You have none of your equipment with you, only a pocket screwdriver and a number of other small odds and ends (eg pocket multimeter, two resistors, insulating tape, two flying leads with banana plug ends) which have accumulated in your pockets since you last turned them out. However, you can see part of the main fuselage of the plane straddled on a reef some 400 yards from the shore, and think it might be possible to get to it and salvage some tools and/or electronic equipment. This could be a risky business. You have no idea what state the plane's wreckage is in, and the waters of this area are notorious for sharks.

VISITORS

Objective   • to introduce concepts of planning and the organisation of group activity

Description   Participants are told that they have to prepare the room for the arrival of four visitors. Given the inadequate nature of this information, the group's assumptions, techniques and achievements will be explored

Target group   Years 1–5 (all abilities)

Organisation   The class can work as a single group with or without observers

or

Groups of 10–12
One tutor per working group

Time required   45 minutes

Tutor Skill   C (see page 17)

Location   Any normal classroom or class working area

Materials   None

Tutor's notes

1. Read the following statement:
   The group/class is to receive four visitors. You have up to 20 minutes in which to plan how to arrange the room for them, and then 5 minutes in which to carry out your planned arrangement.

   (25 minutes)

2. You must be prepared to answer any questions from the group about the purpose, status etc of the visitors, but should not volunteer this information unless it is requested.

3. *Review*
   Groups should be encouraged to consider:

   • the amount of time they put into their planning
   (If they have done nothing of this nature before, it will probably have been very little.)

   • whether they considered (or asked) why the visitors were coming

   • whether they considered different ways in which the room could be arranged (eg for four separate visitors, two pairs, one group)

   • how they organised themselves. Did they have a leader? Who did the work? etc

   (20 minutes)

COMBINED OPERATIONS

Objectives
- to improve planning and communication skills
- to explore the behaviour of groups

Description
The groups in competition are asked to produce a copy of a map or a circuit diagram, following the instructions of their leaders, who are in a separate room. There are stringent limitations on the communication systems that can be set up between the leaders and the groups. As a result a variety of behaviour including frustration, irritation and resentment, is likely to emerge

Target group
Years 3–5, 6th form

Organisation
Groups of 5–6
Two tutors plus observers

Time required
1¼ hours (minimum)

Tutor skill
B (see page 17)

Location
Two rooms in reasonable proximity, preferably with a corridor between them

Materials
For each group:
Two copies of the *Leaders' briefing sheet 1*
Two copies of the *Leaders' briefing sheet 2*
One set of group instructions
One map of Greater Cokington
or One circuit diagram
40 message forms
One in/out-tray with the group's number on it
Pens, pencils, paper

Tutor's notes

1. Establish groups of 5–6. Number all groups. Choose (by any means appropriate) two members of each group as leaders; the remainder are workers. Locate all leaders in one room, all workers in the other. One tutor should be in each room. The in/out-trays (cardboard box or equivalent) should each be labelled with the number of a group and placed outside the leaders' room. (*5 minutes*)

2. Issue *Briefing sheet 1* and message forms to leaders and *Group instruction sheet* to group. The leaders in particular may have questions to ask and may require some guidance, but this should be kept to a minimum. Allow the leaders 5 minutes to prepare for their meetings with their groups. (*10 minutes*)

3. Arrange for leaders to meet their groups in the group room. They may only give their groups oral instructions together with message forms. (*5 minutes*)

4. Issue *Briefing sheet 2* which includes the diagram or map to leaders. Announce the start of the task. Groups work on task. (*about 30 minutes*)

5. Task ends. Check scores. Declare winners. (*5 minutes*)

6. *Review*

Points which should emerge will include:

a *Role of the leader*

- did the leaders make full use of their preliminary meeting with the workers?
- did they give them adequate instructions eg competition, in/out-trays, economy in sending messages, keeping score etc?
- did they carry out their own instructions eg keeping the score; not writing in diagram space on message form; limiting words on message form to 10 etc?
- after receiving *Briefing sheet 2*, did they tell the workers what they were going to do?
- did they make an adequate plan for transmitting the diagram/map?

b *Behaviour of the group*

- did the workers feel they were adequately briefed?
- were they ever left in limbo? What did they do for the first 10 minutes, before their briefing from the leaders?
- what did they do if/when they became frustrated?
- were they aware that they were competing with the others? How did this affect them?
- did they have their own leader? How did he emerge? What effect did he have?
- did they take any initiatives? What?

(*20 minutes*)

COMBINED OPERATIONS
Group instructions

1 Groups are to wait in this room until joined by your leaders who will give you further instructions.

2 You may not leave the room except to collect and deliver messages on the instructions of your leaders.

3 You may only do things which your leaders instruct you to do.

4 Pens, pencils and paper are provided for your use.

COMBINED OPERATIONS
Leader's briefing sheet 1

1 You and your group will shortly be asked to undertake a specific task. In this task you will be competing against the other groups.

2 *Scoring*
   a Each group starts with 1000 points. The group with most points when the task ends is the winner.
   b The first group to complete the task to the tutor's satisfaction gains a further 250 points.
   c Points will be deducted as described in section 3 below.
   d You must keep your group's score, which you may be asked for at any time.

3 *Communication*
   All the groups are together in another room nearby. Communication between you and your group must be limited to written messages on the standard message form. This form has space for a maximum of 10 words and/or a diagram. No words may be written in the diagram space or vice-versa. 15 points will be deducted for each form used.

4 *The task*
   You are allowed 5 minutes to study this brief. You will then have an opportunity to meet your group for a further 3 minutes to give them any instructions you think necessary and to answer any questions. You may not give them anything in writing other than message forms. Your tutor will arrange this meeting for you.
   After this meeting you will be issued with *Briefing sheet 2* which specifies the task to be carried out.

5 *Resources and limitations*
   - Your group is equipped with pens, pencils and paper.
   - At present your group has no information about the exercise at all except that they will receive instructions from you which they must carry out explicitly.
   - An in/out-tray with your group's number on it is located outside this room. Messages to and from your group must be placed in this tray. Under no circumstances may you speak to any group member after your meeting with them ends.
   - You may not leave this room (apart from your initial meeting with your group) except to place messages in the in/out-tray or to collect replies.
   - Only one member of your group (whom you must appoint) may leave their room to visit the in/out-tray.
   - The exercise will end as soon as the first group indicates that it has completed the task and the tutor is satisfied. This indication can only be given by the leaders of that group to the tutor.
   - The tutors will insist that the rules of the exercise are applied strictly at all times.

The task of your group is to produce a copy of this circuit diagram as accurately as possible.

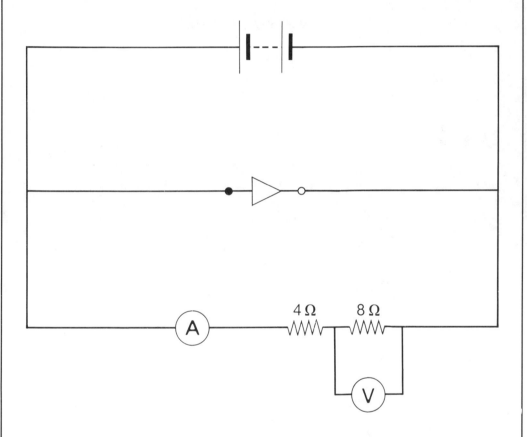

In the circuit shown the reading on the Ammeter is 4A

LEARNING
IN *ACTION*

The task of your group is to produce a copy of this map as accurately as possible.

GREATER COKINGTON

INDUSTRIAL ESTATE

NORTH ST

CIVIC CENTRE

ASHBOROUGH

THE BOULEVARD

EAST ST

RLY

BULL RING

ST

SOUTH ST

RIVER

GASVILLE

GRUBB

COMBINED OPERATIONS
Message Form

LEARNING
IN *ACTION*

From _____

To _____   Message No _____

	1	2	3	4	5
	6	7	8	9	10

COST OF MESSAGE 15 POINTS	FOR DIAGRAMS ETC

ISLANDS IN THE SUN

Objectives
- to improve skills in information retrieval
- to improve skills in joint problem solving

Description   This is a planning exercise involving a holiday in the Greek Islands. The information initially available is inadequate, and the tutor retains much that is essential. This is released only in response to specific requests.

Target group   Years 3–5, 6th form
(This exercise will probably be too complex for the less academic)

Organisation   Groups of 5
One tutor per two groups minimum plus observers

Time required   On-going. The exercise is likely to require several periods and homework or private study

Tutor skill   A (see page 17)

Location   Any room in which groups can work with reasonable privacy

Materials   One briefing sheet per group
Copies of the following information sheets (to be held by the tutor):
ISRA application form (one for each participant)
Greek tourist board information for travellers
Great Western Bank PLC/other sources of funding
Passport Office, Liverpool
Travel Agents
Staff suggestions for research
Map of Greece

Tutor's notes

1. Distribute briefing sheets and ask groups to work on the exercise. Wait for questions/complaints to arise about lack of information

2. When information is requested, release what is asked for, but no more. It is up to the discretion of the tutor to interpret this, and also to decide how much prompting should be given. This clearly will depend on the age and ability of the group

3. *Review*
This will probably centre round three areas:
   a *The solution of the problem*
   - who managed to work out a reasonable scheme?
   b *Information retrieval*
   - how good were the groups at knowing what they needed to find out and where to get the information?
   - were essentials overlooked?
   - how does this relate to everyday life at school and at home?
   c *The behaviour of the group*
   - what was the initial reaction when confronted with the briefing—initiative, bewilderment, frustration?
   - how did the group gain momentum?
   - who were the key figures in this process?

LEARNING IN *ACTION*

You and your friends have always wanted to visit the Greek Islands, but have been prevented from doing so by lack of funds. You had particularly hoped to go during the coming summer holidays (July 25th–September 6th), but the most you can raise is still only about £100 each. Imagine your interest, then, when you see the following notice on the College board:

FOREIGN RESEARCH GRANTS

The International Students Research Association (ISRA) offers 50% grants towards the travel costs and out-of-pocket expenses of bona fide students who wish to undertake vacation research in any of the following areas: Algeria, Australia, Canada, Cyprus, Egypt, EEC Countries, Iceland, India, Israel, Jordan, Morocco, New Zealand, Norway, Sweden, Tunisia, USSR, USA. Further details can be obtained from:

International Students Research Association,
Friendship House,
South Craven Street,
London,
SW1A 4VW

The association thanks you for your enquiry. You are asked to complete the following form. *All questions must be answered.*

1 FULL NAME (or names if more than one in party) and DATE(S) OF BIRTH

_____

_____

_____

2 SCHOOL, COLLEGE OR UNIVERSITY

_____

_____

_____

3 COUNTRY/COUNTRIES TO BE VISITED

_____

_____

_____

4 NATURE OF RESEARCH
(This must be supported by your official tutor)

_____

_____

_____

5 METHOD OF TRAVEL TO COUNTRY OF DESTINATION
(If air or sea, indicate airport of port of departure)

_____

_____

_____

6 DATE OF DEPARTURE

_____

7 DATE OF RETURN

_____

8 METHOD OF INTERNAL TRAVEL ON ARRIVAL

_____

_____

_____

9 TYPE OF ACCOMMODATION SOUGHT

_____

_____

_____

10 ESTIMATES

	£	P.
Travel to country of destination		
Internal travel		
Accommodation		
Food		
Other expenses (specify)		
TOTAL		

NB Total grant available is 50%, up to a maximum of £250.

11 PASSPORT NO(S)

_____

12 TUTOR'S SIGNATURE

....

I declare that the information given in this form was accurate at the time of writing. I am a citizen of the United Kingdom.

Signature (s)   ....

....

....

ISLANDS IN THE SUN
Greek Tourist Board information
for travellers

Accommodation

The country offers a wide variety of places to stay. All hotels and rooms are officially categorised by the Tourist Police. Prices (one person per night) are, on average:

Hotels–Category	A	Dr 3000	Rooms	Dr 975
	B	Dr 2625		
	C	Dr 2250		

Youth Hostels are available in most major towns. The average price is Dr 600 per person per night.
Camping is only allowed at official camping sites. These sites are nationally run and cost Dr 225 per person per night. Tents can be hired for an additional Dr 300 per night.

Food

Food in Greece is good and inexpensive, unless you choose to eat in Category A or B Hotels. There are numerous tavernas offering varied and reasonable menus: major tourist resorts now have fast-food restaurants of high quality. Food shops, super- and mini-markets abound for those who choose to do their own catering. It should be possible to live comfortably on Dr 2000 per head per day.

Travel

Air

Air travel in Greece has opened up vastly during the past few years. There are now airports on Carpathos, Cephalinia, Chios, Corfu, Cos, Crete, Lemnos, Lesbos, Milos, Mykonos, Naxos, Paros, Rhodes, Samos, Santorini, Skiathos and Zante. Flights are inexpensive (in the range Dr 3250–5400 from the islands to Athens), but inter-island travel by air is limited (eg Crete—Santorini—Mykonos). Most flights are by small planes which tend to get booked up well in advance.

Sea

Still the most popular and varied way of travelling between the islands. Boats vary in size from large car ferries to 'Flying Dolphin' hydrofoils and small converted fishing vessels. There is no central booking system for sea travel, each shipping line having its own individual offices and agents in each island. Boats are frequent, but schedules and routes can change, and prices vary according to the type of boat on which you are travelling. It is necessary, therefore, to allow time to check schedules and prices on each island. Allow between Dr 550 and 1600 for each inter-island journey.

Road

Buses and taxis are plentiful in most islands, and motor-bikes and mopeds can be hired from Dr 500 per day. Bus and taxi fares are considerably cheaper than in UK.

NB Inter-island travel can be very time-consuming if you get your itinerary in the wrong order. You are respectfully advised to visit islands basically in the same group.
Maps can be supplied from this Office.

© 1987   Roger Kirk   Basil Blackwell

The Bank offered the following facilities:

1 Travel cheques and foreign currency
2 Eurocheques
3 Travel insurance
4 Holiday 'Saver-Scheme'
5 Credit card (Credit guarantee essential)
6 Help with holiday budgeting

In reply to specific enquiries, the following replies were given:

1 Exchange rate—Dr 200 = £1
2 Passports—enquiries about individual or group passports should be made to The Passport Office, Liverpool.
3 Medical Care—to obtain free or subsidised treatment while in any EEC country, you will need to produce a certificate of entitlement (Form E111) which can be obtained from a local DHSS office.

ISLANDS IN THE SUN
Other sources of funding

Information from Head, Head of Year, Form Tutor etc.

1 *LEA* In the present financial climate grants are rare, but on occasions up to £50 can still be obtained if need can be proved.

2 *Emily Barton Trust* Money left under the will of the late Emily Cecilia Barton to help with the education of children in need living in the area. Need still has to be proved, and the Trustees generally require evidence that applicants (and their parents, where relevant) are making as great a contribution to costs as they can afford. No upper limit, but grants of more than £250 are rare.

3 *Governor's Discretionary Awards* The Governors of the College usually make two Awards of £25 a year for projects of individual pupils which show particular imagination or enterprise.

ISLANDS IN THE SUN
Passport Office, Liverpool

LEARNING IN *ACTION*

1 *Individual passports*

Application forms for individual passports can be obtained from the Passport Office, Liverpool, or from your nearest General Post Office. The form must be submitted to the Passport Office, together with two photographs and the remittance of £15. Your passport is valid for 10 years.

2 *Group passports*

Group passports can be issued for groups of up to 50 young people under 17 years of age, accompanied by two adults who travel on their own passports. Application forms can be obtained from the Passport Office, Liverpool, your nearest General Post Office or your Travel Agent. No photographs are required and the remittance is £14 for the group.

You are advised that some countries also require identity cards. Details of these countries will be supplied by the Passport Office.

1 *Air Zeus*
Daily flights from Heathrow

Economy class single fares

Length of stay in Greece

Destination	Flights	1 night	7	14	28
		£	£	£	£
Athens	Daily	405	316	228	156
Thessaloniki	Daily	424	335	247	175
Heraklion	M,W	430	344	256	182
Corfu	Tu, F	393	304	216	144

2 *Siberian Airlines*
Charter flights from Gatwick

Return fares

Destination	Flights		March–April	May–June; Sept–Oct	July–August
	April May Sept Oct	June July August	£	£	£
Athens	W,F	M,W,F	123	135	149
Chania	W,F	M,W,F	137	151	166
Rhodes	Tu	Tu,Th	149	164	180
Kos	Th	Tu,Th	158	184	202

3 *Freesun Holidays*
Charter flights from Manchester

Return fares

Destination	Flights			April-October	May-September	June, July August
	Apr. May June	July August	September October	£	£	£
Corfu	Sa,Su	Daily	Sa,Su,W	119	125	131
Santorini	M	M,F	M	164	172	180
Mykonos	Tu	Tu,F	F	199	209	214
Skiathos	M	M,Th	Th	193	201	206
Zante	W	Tu,W	Tu	154	161	165

1 Mr Monument (Classics)

Crete is a 'must'. In addition to Knossos, there are important sites at Tylissos, Gortyn, Phaistos, Ayia Triadha, Mallia, Gournia and Zakro with excellent museums.

Delos, the birthplace of Apollo and Artemis, was the religious and political centre of ancient Greece, and French archaeologists have and are discovering amazing finds. At least two visits are necessary, which is tricky as there is no accommodation on the island and you will have to stay on Mykonos.

Santorini has a fine Minoan site at Akrotiri and its ancient capital, Thera, both well worth a visit. You may want to visit Ithaka though there are not many traces of Odysseus there now. Rhodes contains the magnificent acropolis at Lindos; Kameiros is worth a visit, but there is not much left at Ialysos. There are other sites worth exploring on Samos and Kos, but really, with the exceptions of Crete and Delos, you would make better use of your time on the mainland.

2 Mrs Lavender (Biology)

Waxed eloquent about the flora of Greece, of which there at least 6000 species, nearly 10% of which are endemic. The island of Crete, for instance, though 35 times smaller than Britain, has over 2000 species, almost the same number as Britain. Genera such as *Dianthus*, *Viola*, *Campanula*, *Gentaurea* and *Colchium* are each represented by several hundred species. Anywhere in Greece is worth visiting; Rhodes and Crete among the larger islands, and Zante and Cythera among the smaller, are outstanding. Best season—the spring or autumn; not much to be seen in August.

She wasn't quite so knowledgeable about the fauna though she spoke of dolphins to be seen, especially in the straits between Naxos and Paros; of the butterflies of Paros and Rhodes (this latter island is also a haven for snakes and lizards); of the wild tortoises in Corfu; and of Lesbos, which contains the very rare star shrew, the salamander and herds of wild horses.

Birds are better on the mainland. But the islands hold a good collection of birds of prey and warblers (eg Orphean, Sardinian, olive-tree) which would not be seen in Britain. Sea birds included shearwaters and pelicans.

3 Mr Sprint (PE)

Knew about sailing in the Ionian islands, skiing in Crete and windsurfing almost anywhere, but doubted whether this would count as research.

4 Miss Castle (History)

There was so much medieval history about that she did not know where to begin. Most islands had something to offer, but pride of place obviously went to Rhodes with its extensive remains from the times of the Knights Templar, including the complete city walls 2½ miles in length. There was also in Rhodes some good Islamic architecture.

She also strongly recommended the Venetian town in Corfu, of which much survives in good condition, and the 19th century Royal Palace.

5 Mrs Humble (RE)

Suggested ikons and monasteries.

6 Mr Mapp (Geography)

Thought the whole idea was a waste of time.

7 Miss Craggs (Geology)

Obviously much study could be done as Greece is a geological goldmine like so many volcanic areas. Santorini, for instance, is a huge volcano of which the centre disappeared in prehistoric times in a vast explosion. There is still volcanic action about, and many of the beaches consist of black sand. Islands such as Kos, Lemnos and Cythnos still abound with hot springs.

There are extremely interesting opportunities for research into minerals, especially in Milos where sulphur, alum, obsidian, bentonite, barium, porlite and kaolin have been mined in times past. Paros still contains the famous marble quarries of ancient times, and Ithaca, Corfu, Anti-Paros and Crete all have fine caves. In addition, of course, Crete contains the Gorge of Samaria, 11 miles long and said to be the longest true gorge in Europe. It is nearly 300 metres deep, sheer, and at times its walls are only a few metres apart. Another notable feature of the area is the many solution notches and faults. These are especially noticeable in Aegina and Spetsai.

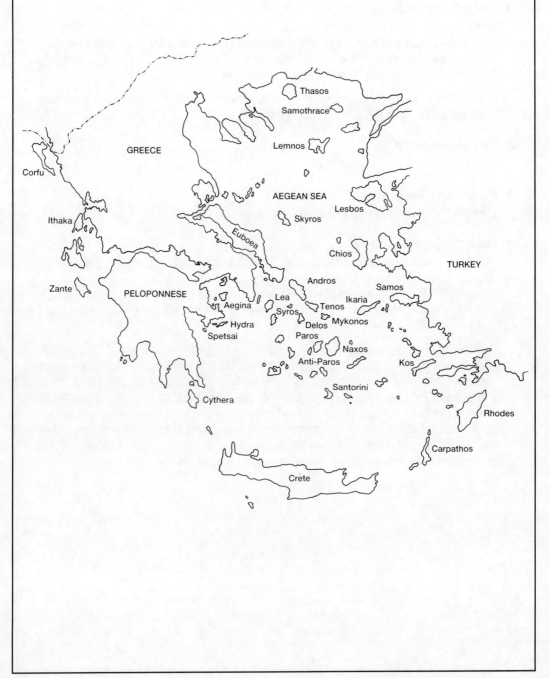

ISLANDS IN THE SUN
Map

Thasos

Samothrace

GREECE

Lemnos

Corfu

AEGEAN SEA

Lesbos

Ithaka

Skyros

Euboea

Chios

TURKEY

Andros

Zante

Samos

PELOPONNESE

Lea

Ikaria

Aegina

Tenos

Syros

Mykonos

Hydra

Delos

Spetsai

Paros

Naxos

Anti-Paros

Kos

Santorini

Cythera

Rhodes

Carpathos

Crete

RAFFLE

Objective	• to develop skills in planning, co-operation and communication
Description	Two groups in separate rooms are asked to plan how they will produce raffle tickets and to write their plans in detail on a blackboard or flip-chart. The groups then change rooms and are required to put into practice each other's plans
Target group	Pupils (all ages and abilities)
Organisation	Two groups of 6–8 One tutor per group plus observers (the exercise can easily be extended to three or four groups)
Time required	1¼ hours (minimum)
Tutor skill	B (see page 17)
Location	A room for each group, one room must be large enough for plenary session. A blackboard or flip-chart is needed in each room
Materials	*For each group:* 1 briefing sheet 1 pair scissors 1 ruler 1 roll sellotape 4 felt-tip pens (different colours) 30 sheets foolscap paper, preferably plain (this can be scrap provided one side can be written on) 10 paper clips (Some of these materials (eg sellotape and paper clips) have no perceived use and are intended as distractions. They can be added to, if required.)

Tutor's notes

1. Divide the class into two groups of 6–8. The groups must be in separate rooms. Issue each group with briefing sheet and a set of the materials outlined above. (*5 minutes*)
2. Groups work on their plans. (It is up to individual groups to decide details of the raffle, such as whether it is private or public.) (*25 minutes*)
3. Instruct the groups to change rooms and carry out the plan they find described on the blackboard. (*15 minutes*)
4. *Review*
   General discussion in plenary, which should include the following points:
   • which plan was more effective? Why?
   • did the plan as described on the blackboard contain all the necessary information and instructions?
   • if not, what was missing?
   • did the plan contain sufficient information about details— arrangement of the room for working; individual tasks; allocation of materials; design of tickets, counterfoils etc. . ?
   • what lessons have been learned about planning?—about communicating?
   (*30 minutes*)

Your group has decided to run a raffle in aid of charity. The prize is to be a large teddy bear, presented by Kudlitoys of Leeds Ltd, and the tickets will be 10p each. The draw will be on Friday, _____ 21st.

In order to save costs and to make the maximum profit for the charity, you have decided to manufacture your own raffle tickets. Your immediate task is to plan how to design and make 500 raffle tickets with the materials available from your tutor, as quickly as possible.

Your plan is to be written up on the blackboard and must be in sufficient detail to be clearly understood and acted upon by anyone coming into the room or joining the group. Do not attempt to carry out your plan until you are given instructions to do so. You have 25 minutes in which to complete your plan.

THE GO-BETWEEN

Objectives	• to study communication skills
	• to explore the behaviour of groups
	• to examine the role and effect of intermediaries
Description	The groups in competition are asked to produce a copy of a map or circuit diagram following the instructions of their leaders who are in a separate room. There are stringent limitations on the communication system that can be set up between leaders and groups. As a result a variety of behaviour, including frustration, irritation and resentment, is likely to emerge.
Target group	Staff and 6th form
Organisation	Groups of 5
	2 tutors, plus observers
Time required	1½ hours (minimum)
Tutor skill	A (see page 17)
Location	Two rooms in reasonable proximity, preferably with a corridor between them
Materials	*For each group:*
	One copy of *Leader's briefing sheet 1*
	One copy of *Leader's briefing sheet 2*
	One copy of group instructions
	One map of Whitham on Sea
	or One circuit diagram
	One Form AB3
	25 Forms AB1 (white)
	10 Forms AB2 (coloured)
	Pens, pencils, paper
	One in/out-tray with the group's number on it

Tutor's notes

1. Establish groups of 5. Number all groups. Get each group to choose a leader and each leader to choose a runner. Locate all leaders and their runners in one room, all others in another. The in/out-trays (cardboard box or equivalent) should each be labelled with the number of the group and placed outside the leaders' room. One tutor must be in each room. (*5 minutes*)

2. Issue *Briefing sheet 1* and *Forms AB1* and *AB3* to leaders, and *Group instruction sheets* to groups. Pens, pencils, paper and copies of *Form AB2* should be placed in the groups' room. Work through the sheets if necessary and answer any questions. (*5 minutes*)

3. Leaders use *Form AB3* if they wish. (*5 minutes*)

4. Issue *Briefing sheet 2* and map or circuit diagram to leaders. Announce the start of the task. Groups work on the task. Tutors need to check the number of messages each group sends and receives by runner. (*about 45 minutes*)

D

5. Task ends. Check scores. Declare winner. (*5 minutes*)
6. *Review*

Points to emerge from discussion should include:

a Problems of communciation/the role of the runner

- did the leader make full and good use of *Form AB3?*
- did he tell the group what they were going to do?
- did he give adequate instructions—competition; in-trays; sparing use of *AB2*, etc?
- how did he decide when to use written messages and when to use the runner?
- did he make a good plan for transmitting the map/diagram?
- did he carry out his own instructions—keeping score, not writing in diagram space on *AB1*, limiting messages on *AB1* to 10 words, etc?
- was he tempted to win by doing nothing—losing no points?
- how much initiative was taken by the runner?
- did the runner distort or forget messages?

b Behaviour of the group

- did the group feel they were adequately briefed?
- were they ever left in limbo?
- what did they do if/when they became frustrated?
- were they aware they were competing with others in the room? How did this affect them?
- did they appoint their own leader or did one emerge? What effect did this have?
- did they take any initiatives? What?
- how did they perceive the runner? What was their relationship with him?

c Relationship to the school/college situation

- what parallels can be seen between this exercise and everyday communication and behaviour in school/college?
- how did the role of the runner compare with that of a Deputy?

1 You may only do things which your leader instructs you to do.

2 You may not leave this room except to deliver and collect messages on the instructions of your leader.

3 Pens, pencils, paper and copies of *Form AB2* are provided for your use.

1 You and your group will shortly be asked to undertake a specific task in which you will be competing against the other groups.

2 *Scoring*

a Each group starts with 1000 points. The group with most points when the task ends is the winner.

b The first group to complete the task to the tutor's satisfaction gains a further 500 points.

c Points will be deducted as described in section 3 below.

d You must keep your group's score, which you may be asked for at any time.

3 *Communication*

All the groups are together in another room nearby. Communication between you and your group is limited to the following:

a Verbal messages via your runner. Your runner may convey oral messages, engage in discussion with the group, and bring back their reply. On no account may the runner write anything down, or carry or handle any written or other material. Each round trip by your runner between you and the group (including the return) 'costs' 100 points.

b Written messages on the forms provided. There are three message forms available:

AB1 For you to communicate with your group.
Each form has space for a maximum of 10 words and/or a diagram. However, no words may be written in the diagram space or vice versa.
Each form used costs 25 points.

AB2 For your group to communicate with you.
Each form has space for a maximum of 10 words but no diagram
Each form used costs 50 points

AB3 For your use in the first 5 minutes of the exercise
There is no limit to the information transmitted and no cost is incurred.

4 *The task*

You are allowed 5 minutes to study this brief and to send your group any instructions you think necessary on *Form AB3*. This will be delivered to your group for you by the tutor. You will then be issued with *Briefing sheet 2*, which specifies the task to be carried out.

5 *Resources and limitations*

- Pens, pencils, paper and copies of *Form AB2* are available in the group room.

- At present your group has no information about the exercise at all except that they will receive instructions from you which they must carry out explicitly.

- An in/out-tray with your group's number on it is located outside this room. Written messages to and from your group must be placed in this tray. Under no circumstances may you speak to any group member.

- You may not leave this room except to place messages in the in/out-tray or to collect replies.

© 1987   Roger Kirk   Basil Blackwell

THE GO-BETWEEN
Leader's briefing

THE GO-BETWEEN
Leader's briefing sheet 1 *continued*

- Only one member of your group (whom you must designate) may leave their room to visit the in/out-tray.
- The exercise will end as soon as the first group indicates that it has completed the task and the tutor is satisfied. This indication can only be given by the leader of that group to the tutor.
- The tutors will insist that the rules of the exercise are applied strictly at all times.

The task of your group is to produce a copy of this map as close to your original as possible.

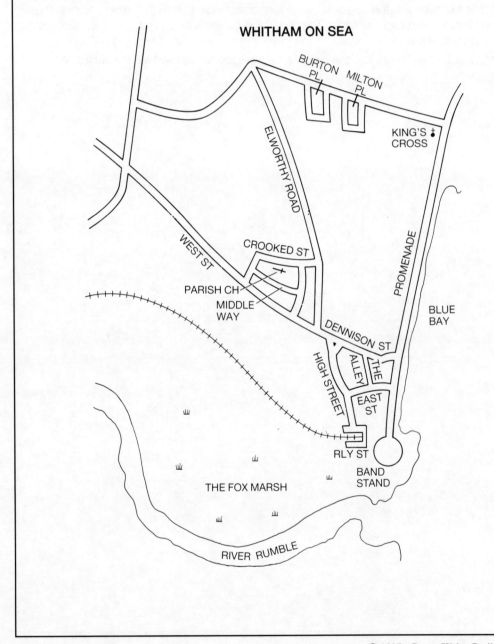

WHITHAM ON SEA

The task of your group is to produce a copy of this circuit diagram as close to your original as possible.

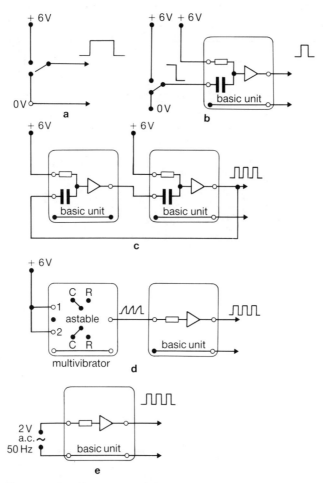

Five ways of making square pulses
a Switch
b Basic unit as a pulse producer
c Two basic units as a slow astable
d Fast astable, squared with a basic unit
e Basic unit squaring a sinusoidal input

THE GO-BETWEEN
Message Form AB1

From _____

To Group _____

Message No _____

	1	2	3	4	5
	6	7	8	9	10

COST OF MESSAGE 25 POINTS	FOR DIAGRAMS ETC

THE GO-BETWEEN
Message Form AB2

From Group _____

To _____

Message No _____

	1	2	3	4	5
	6	7	8	9	10

COST OF MESSAGE—50 POINTS

THE GO-BETWEEN
Message Form AB3

FROM _____   TO GROUP _____

FAMILY BUSINESS

Objective • to help young people improve personal presentation, and to consider the relevance of specific skills, qualities and qualifications for specific jobs

Description Participants have to select from letters of application the most suitable candidate for a job in the 'family business'.

Target group Years 3–5 (all abilities), CPVE students

Organisation Groups of 4–6
One tutor

Time required 1–1¼ hours

Tutor skill C (see page 17)

Location Any room in which groups can work with reasonable privacy

Materials One briefing sheet per pupil
One copy of the job advertisement per group
One set of letters of application (6 in total) per group (these will need regular checking for dates, qualifications etc and revising as necessary)

Tutor's notes

1. Issue the groups with the necessary briefing sheet, advertisements and letters of application.

2. Groups work on their task. (*30–45 minutes*)

3. Groups announce their decisions and compare results.

4. *Review*
   This should highlight the reasons for groups coming to different decisions (if they have). Groups should be asked to consider how much attention they paid to:

   • the difficulties confronting employers in selection

   • style and layout of the letters

   • relevance of the content to the advertisement

   • importance (if any) of examination results and grades; past experience; interests. . .

   • impressions of and deductions about personal qualities

   • missing evidence

   • the subjective nature of selection procedures

   Opportunities to examine group behaviour are limited, but considerations should be given to:

   • how the groups handled the information they had been given

   • how they structured their meetings

   (*15–30 minutes*)

You are one of the partners in a long-established family grocery business with three shops in Chesterfield. You are looking for a new trainee assistant, preferably someone capable of being taken into the partnership in due course, as you are expecting a number of retirements in the next few years.

In response to an advert in the Chesterfield Mercury you have had six letters of application, and you are now meeting with the other partners to decide which one of the applicants you would like to interview first. You do not wish to spend valuable time inverviewing more than one if that can be avoided.

Your group has 40 mins in which to reach a decision and you must be able to give valid reasons for your choice.

FAMILY BUSINESS
Job advertisement

LEARNING
IN *ACTION*

TRAINEE ASSISTANT

Required as soon as possible, a young man or woman to help in a small family grocery business (three outlets) in the Chesterfield area. The immediate duties will include serving in the shops, stock control, delivery, accounting and cleaning. There is the possibility of a partnership in the firm in due course for a suitably qualified applicant. Starting salary £45 per week, overtime available, other conditions to be negotiated.

Letters of application stating age, details of school career, interests etc: as soon as possible to Box 24, Chesterfield Mercury.

LEARNING
IN *ACTION*

Home Manor
Tipley Regis
Derbyshire
DY6 4QQ

24.10.85

Dear Sir,

 I am applying for the post of Trainee Assistant
advertised in the Chesterfield Mercury this week.
My curriculum vitae is attached.

 I have been awarded a place to read Mechanical
Engineering at King's College, Durham for October
1986, and my father, a Director of Multiflex
International Ltd., feels it would be advisable for
me to gain some commercial experience in the mean-
while. I would certainly welcome the contrast with
my comparatively sheltered private school education
to date.

                    Yours faithfully,

                    Jonathan Fortescue

                    (J.P.T. Fortescue)

CURRICULUM VITAE

JONATHAN PIERS TREMAYNE FORTESCUE

Date of birth: 12 May 1967

Home Address: Home Manor, Tipley Regis, Derbyshire DY6 4QQ
                 (Tel: Tipley (00812) 444)

Education: 1 Norton Crest Preparatory School
               Middlewick   1974 - 80

             2 St Matthew's College, Milchester
                                          1980 - 85
               (Head Boy 1984 -5; Captain of Squash;
               President of Drama Club and of
               Bacchanalian Society)

Examination Results:

'O' Level:

English Language	B	English Literature	B
History	C	Geography	B
Mathematics	A	French	C
Physics	A	Spanish	C
Chemistry	A	Latin	B
Biology	A	Religious Education	E

'A' Level:

Physics	A
Chemistry	B
Mathematics	A

Interests: Theatre, golf, motor rallying, field sports,
             foreign travel, sailing

17, Eastfields
Chesterfield
Derbyshire
23 September 1985

Dear Sir

My name is Mandy Hamilton, I would like to apply for the post of Trainee Assistant at your shop. I am 18 years of age.

For the last two years I have been studying catering at Bakewell Technical College. Even though I have passed the course I have been unable to find a job.

I was a pupil at Fallowfields Comprehensive School where I got CSE in Typing (2), Cookery (2), General Science (5), and Art (3). While I was at school I was part of the tuck-shop team, serving in the shop and counting the money.

While on my course I have worked as a waitress and in the kitchens and when I was at school I worked on Saturday mornings in the bread bakers and confectioners.

My interests are TV, ice-skating, music, hair-dressing and motor bikes. I can type. My favourite pop star is Boy George.

Please would you give me a chance. I am desperately keen to have a job and would be prepared to be on trial or to take a lower wage.

Yours faithfully

Mandy Hamilton

Mandy Hamilton

                                        Sylvan Cottage
                                        Little Wanford
                                        Nr Chesterfield
                                        DY4 8ZA

                                        23.9.85

Dear Sir
   I am writing to apply for the post of Traine Assistant as
advertised in the Chesterfield Mercury. I enclose a curriculum
vitae which includes the names of appropriate referees.

   Although I have only just left school, I have had three
years experience with a paper round and have also had a
regular job at the week-end since I was 11 at the local
stables. My grandparents own a business which sound's
similar to yours in Grantham, and I always help them out
when I am staying with them.

   I left school in order to take up nursing or go into the
forces, but they will not take me on till I am 18. I am
very interested in your job and would not mind making
my career in it instead.

                        Yours sincerely

                        Sophie Ashford

                        Sophie Ashford

Curriculum Vitae

Name   Sophie Elizabeth Ashford

Address   Sylvan Cottage
            Little Wansford
            Nr Chesterfield DY4 8ZA

Date of Birth   21st October 1968·

Education   Fallowfields Comprehensive School
             Chesterfield   1978 - 85

Exam Results   'O' level

                English (C), Religious Education (C)

                CSE Maths (5)   Geography (1)
                     Chemistry (5) Office Practice (2)
                     Childcare (2) Typing (U)

School activities   Hockey Under 16 team
                    Netball Under 16 team
                    Tennis Under 16 team
                    Social service group
                    School choir

Other interests   Guides
                   Church choir
                   Pony Club
                   Fashion
                   Sport
                   Music

Referees

1 The Headmaster   2 Mr B Rogers
  Fallowfields Compre-   Blacklow Stables, Piggery
  hensive School,   Lane, Little Wansford,
  Chesterfield   Nr Chesterfield DY4 8GK

LEARNING
IN *ACTION*

Miss E. M. Hughes
33 Station Road
Loxworth
Chesterfield
Derby
30th September

Dear Sir

I am 19 years of age and am at present on the check-out at Savewell supermarket in Draytown where I have been working for the past year. Before that I spent nine months helping in the home of Dr. Ann Rushton of Cockebridge, where I helped with the children and did general housework.

I was a pupil at Loxworth Comprehensive school where I gained these examination results :-

'O' level - English Lang (C), Art (C), Social Studies(E)
CSE - Office Practice (2), French (3), Biology (3),
        Home Economics (5).

I then spent one year in the 6th form where I took and gained certificate of Pre-Vocational Education. At school I was a librarian. Also I was a member of the school orchestra. I was secretary of the school council and belonged to the chess club. My other interests are tennis, reading, camping and photography.

For four years while at school I helped an old lady with her shopping. Now most of my free time is spend helping out at home as my mother suffers from multiple sterosis.

Dr. Rushton and the Manager of Savewell supermarket are my referees.

yours faithfully
E. M. Hughes
(MISS E. M. HUGHES)

3 West Street
Chesterfield
DY3 4WA.
26th September
1985.

Dear Sir,

Please would you consider me for your recently advertised post of Trainee Assistant.

I am 17 years old and was educated at Fallowfields Comprehensive School. While there I played for the schools football and cricket teams, and gained the following results at CSE Maths (1), English (2), Design (2), Physics (3), Geography (5), French (U). I did not take any 'O' levels. Last September I went into 6th form but found it did not suite me, so I left school at Christmas. Since then I have been working on my uncle's farm at Duggesby, but am looking for something more interesting and with better prospects.

In the past I have had a paper round and have helped on Saturday mornings on my father's van. My father works for EP Forsdyke (Provisions) Ltd and is manager of their Bark Street Branch. I am a Sgt. in the ACF and am interested in music, BMX bikes and judo.

If you employ me you will find that I am hard-working, punctual, tidy and well-behaved. I am happy to come to an interview at any time.

Yours sincerely
Mr. Peter Dawson.

178 Cheviot Street
Chesterfield,
DY1 7FT.

Dear Sir,

I am interested in the job of trainee asistant I left school in march this year and since have worked as a ~~bric~~ brick layer asistant groundsman and looking after chikens. I need the money for my pidgeons.

Wayne Cook

JORDAN HOMES LTD

Objective

- to examine the principles of 'selling' and 'buying' and how a school or college can 'sell' itself, its objectives, its courses etc.

Description

An exercise in presentation and image building. Participants are either house purchasers or sales representatives. Their interaction centres on the purchase of optional extras for a recently purchased property

Target group

Staff

Organisation

Groups of 8–10
One/two tutors plus observers

Time required

1½ hours (minimum)

Tutor skill

A (see page 17)

Location

A room or rooms big enough to permit a plenary session; two groups meeting in reasonable privacy; 4–5 individual negotiations

Materials

Accessories list for all participants
Purchaser's brief for all purchasers
For all representatives:
Representative's brief
Commission sheet
Purchaser's contract

Tutor's notes

1. Divide the group into Representatives and Purchasers. Issue the appropriate briefing sheets, accessories lists etc.

2. Representatives and Purchasers confer separately. The aim of each group is to establish a common course of action for the coming negotiations. (*20 minutes*)

3. Partner each of the Reps with one of the Purchasers. They now have to negotiate their sales and sign a purchaser's contract. (*30 minutes*)

4. Representatives and Purchasers return to their respective groups to discuss

   - their success at selling or buying

   - their ability to adhere to the proposed common course of action

   (*20 minutes*)

5. *Review*

   This should focus mainly on consideration of the relevance of the exercise to the concept of 'selling' a school or college or its products. Points which should emerge will include:

   - did the purchasers decide what they would rather have?

   - did they try to predict what the reps would try to sell?

   - did they want to be persuaded?

   - did they suspect the reps' openness, honesty and motive?

   - did the representatives take full account of profit margin, discount, commission etc?

- did they predict what they would succeed in selling?
- were they committed to what they were trying to sell?
- what were the freedoms?
- what were the perceived constraints? Were they real or imaginary?

(*20 minutes*)

6. This exercise can be easily modified or extended by the tutor in a number of ways eg

   a setting up more 'freedoms' by *not* requiring meetings to take place either between Reps or Purchasers.

   b giving Purchasers the opportunity of comparing the offers of different Reps.

   c providing cost information to Reps for *their* transmission to the Purchasers etc.

You have just completed the purchase (from Jordan Homes Ltd) of a select new bungalow (costing £61,950) on an exclusive 'village' estate.

Each of this new range of bungalows, called *Riverside*, is fully centrally heated, with ample garden and a double garage. It comprises a lobby, hallway and cloakrooms; separate living room and dining room, both with patio windows into the garden; kitchen with split level oven/hob and utility room; master bedroom with bath en suite; two other bedrooms each with hand basin; and a principal bathroom with bidet.

Jordan Homes offer a range of accessories; a price list is attached. Their representative is to call shortly. You are anxious to make purchases from this list but are only able to spend a further £2000. You therefore decide to meet with fellow purchasers of bungalows on the estate to discuss the prices you have been sent, the possibility of obtaining discount, and the tactics to adopt when meeting Jordan Homes' representative. You are anxious to obtain the best bargain possible.

Stage 1
Discuss the line to be followed with your fellow purchasers. Agree a common course of action. (*20 minutes*)

Stage 2
Meet individually with the representative of Jordan Homes and make the best bargain of which you are capable. Complete a 'Purchaser's contract'. (*30 minutes*)

Stage 3
Reconvene with your fellow purchasers to see who has completed the most successful bargain and how closely you were able to adhere to your proposed common course of action. (*20 minutes*)

© 1987 Roger Kirk Basil Blackwell

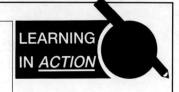

**JORDAN HOMES LTD
Accessories currently available for the
'Riverside' bungalow**

**LEARNING
IN *ACTION***

External	£
Paved garden terrace (8m × 5m)	1250.00
Ornamental fishpond (with fountain)	275.00
Water supply to garage	15.50
Inspection pit	165.00
Exterior 'Ancient Gas' lamp (2m standard)	58.50
Intruder alarm	425.00

Internal	
Extractor fan (kitchen or bathroom)	32.00
Microwave	237.50
Shower (Readiflow De Luxe)	157.00
Loft ladder (fitted)	60.00
Indoor TV aerial	45.50
Breakfast bar (seats 4) with stools	438.00
Wall lights (Kandlglo double bracket) each	13.95
Double glazing (complete house)	1360.00
'Rockwool' cavity insulation	750.00

All prices include VAT and installation charge

You are a sales representative for Jordan Homes Ltd. In the past few months you have been fully involved in the promotion of the *Riverside* bungalow (£61,950), the company's select new range on an exclusive 'village' estate.

The *Riverside* is fully centrally heated with ample garden and a double garage. It comprises a lobby, hallway and cloakroom; separate living room and dining room, both with patio windows into the garden; kitchen with split level oven/hob and utility room; master bedroom with bath en suite; two other bedrooms each with hand basin; and a principal bathroom with bidet.

Your basic salary is only £5,750 p.a., so you rely heavily on any commission you can acquire to make up your income. In particular you depend on making sales from the list of accessories which is attached.

You are about to visit a client, who has just completed the purchase of a *Riverside*, to discuss with him possible purchases from the accessories list. Before this appointment you decide to hold a meeting with fellow reps to discuss ways in which your commission can be maximised.

Stage 1
Discuss the line to be followed with your fellow representatives. Agree a common course of action. (*20 minutes*)

Stage 2
Meet individually with the purchaser and make the best sales of which you are capable. Complete a 'Purchaser's contract'. (*30 minutes*)

Stage 3
Reconvene with your fellow representatives to see who has been the most successful and how closely you were able to adhere to your proposed common course of action. (*20 minutes*)

CONFIDENTIAL

JORDAN HOMES LTD

Sales commission on accessories for the Riverside *bungalow*

External

Paved garden terrace (8m × 5m)	Nil
Ornamental fishpond (with fountain)	50%
Water supply to garage	Nil
Inspection pit	Nil
Exterior 'Ancient Gas' lamp (2m standard)	22.5%
Intruder alarm	17.5%

Internal

Extractor fan (kitchen or bathroom)	9%
Microwave	17.5%
Shower (Readiflow De Luxe)	9%
Loft ladder (fitted)	5%
Indoor TV aerial	Nil
Breakfast bar (seats 4) with stools	20%
Wall lights (Kandlglo double bracket)	33.3%
Double glazing (complete house)	20%
'Rockwool' cavity insulation	15%

JORDAN HOMES LTD
Purchaser's contract

DATE

ITEM PURCHASED   PRICE

TOTAL

Signed ....   Signed ....
(for Jordan Homes Ltd.)   (for Purchaser)

ORANGE MARKET

Objective	• to enable pupils to examine the methods and problems of 'selling' themselves and their skills
	• to enable staff to examine the methods and problems of 'selling' the school or college
Description	An exercise in presentation and image-building. Groups are required to compete with each other in persuading a 'customer' to buy their product in preference to that of their rivals. The product is an orange.
Target group	Pupils (all ages and abilities) and staff
Organisation	Groups of 4–6
	One/two tutors per class and observers
Time required	1–1¼ hours
Tutor skill	C (see page 17)
Location	One room per group or any room in which groups can work with reasonable privacy
Materials	One orange per group
	(Fee/prize for winning group?)

Tutor's notes

1. Divide the class into groups of 4–6. Provide each group with an orange, preferably one with a blemish. All oranges should be of similar size and quality.

2. Read out the following:
   'Each group has been provided with an orange, which it is the aim of the group to sell. A potential purchaser (Name.........................) will be visiting you in 30 minutes time, but he only intends to make one purchase and will buy the orange which appeals to him most. Your task is to ensure in any way you like that it is your orange that he selects'.

   The tutor may be asked questions about price. As this is a 'selling' problem, it is clearly up to the participants to determine this. (*30 minutes + 10 minutes minimum for judging*)

3. *Review*
   Groups should be encouraged to consider:

   • whether they examined the orange before trying to sell it

   • the nature of the target audience; did they try to find out what the purchaser wanted?

   • sales philosophy—description, features, benefit

   • ethical considerations: the relationship between 'selling' and 'conning'

   • the various options open—packaging; brochure; written description; verbal presentation; financial considerations—price; discount (bribery). . .

   • coping with the blemish—does one acknowledge it?—attempt to hide it?—claim it as a benefit?

- the nature of the sales presentation—length; credibility; price etc.
- the relationship of this exercise to 'selling' oneself at interview or to 'selling' one's services in other ways

    (*30 minutes*)

4. This exercise can be varied and its learning can be made more complex by giving the groups oranges of different size or quality.

HORSE OF THE YEAR

Objectives	• to improve joint problem-solving skills • to emphasise the importance of sharing information
Description	The group is required to choose a suitable pony for its purposes from a number which are advertised for sale. Each participant holds some of the data essential to making the correct choice. Once the data is properly shared the right answer will emerge.
Target group	Years 4–5, CPVE students
Organisation	Groups of 5 One/two tutors plus observers
Time required	45 minutes–1 hour
Tutor skill	C (see page 17)
Location	Any room in which groups can work with reasonable privacy
Materials	One briefing sheet for each member of the group. (Sheets are in sets of five, all slightly different but apparently the same. For the tutor's benefit they can be distinguished by the number of full stops at the end of the first paragraph ., .., ..., ..., ...) One *Horses and Ponies for Sale* list per group

Tutor's notes

1. Divide the class into groups of 5. Distribute briefing sheets and *Horses and Ponies for Sale* list. (*5 minutes*)

2. Groups complete exercise. (*25 minutes*)

3. *Review*
   Points to be raised:
   - how long did it take individuals to realise that each briefing sheet was different?
   - how did they then pool their information?
   - did they get the right answer? (see below).
   - did they tackle the problem effectively?
   - how did they allocate responsibilities—leadership; recording etc?
   (*20 minutes*)

4. *Solution*
   Cornflake is the only horse to fulfil all five requirements: height, age, price, sex, temperament. The others are all eliminated on the following grounds:

Singing Nun	—	price, sex
Snowball	—	height
Captain	—	height, sex, temperament
Blue Beaver	—	age, price
Alderney	—	temperament
Jolly Jo	—	age

   While Snowball and Alderney are within the total amount of money the group has (£705), they are excluded if £30 has to be spent on a vet's inspection fee

LEARNING
IN *ACTION*

Singing Nun
Attractive 14 hands 2in Skewbald mare, 10 years, good to catch, shoe, clip and box.
Sadly outgrown. £950
Tel: Summersby 267

Cornflake
Good looking dun gelding, 14 hands 3in. 9 years.
Well schooled, no vices.
Lack of work forces sale. £675
Tel: Stockton 47314

Snowball
13 hands 3in thoroughbred grey gelding. 9 years. Super temperament, 100% traffic.
Genuine reason for sale. £700
Tel: 01 443 4242

Captain
17 hands black stallion, 8 years. Excellent jumper, suit confident competitive teenager.
Rugs included, tack extra. £750
Tel: Sheffield 25713

Blue Beaver
Super looking 14 hands 2in grey gelding. 15 years old. Lovely temperament, suit teenager
or nervous mum. Rider sadly outgrown. £500
Tel: 07499 111

Alderney
15 hands pretty bay gelding, 7 years. Not novice ride. £700
Tel: Maidenhead 6929

Jolly Jo
15 hands 1in chestnut gelding, 5 year old. Ideal for teenager, 100% in every way,
experienced pc activities. Needs kind home urgently. £650
Tel: Ipswich 34187

© 1987   Roger Kirk   Basil Blackwell

HORSE OF THE YEAR
Briefing sheet

LEARNING
IN *ACTION*

Together with four of your friends you have decided to buy a horse or pony for your joint use. You have met to study the 'For Sale' columns of the *Horseman's Weekly* to decide which horse you will buy.

You are an inexperienced rider but your sister who rides regularly has warned you on no account to buy an animal less than 6 years old. You must remember also that a horse of from 14.2 to 15.2 hands will need at least an acre of land to feed on, even if it is a good doer. By asking relatives for money for recent Christmas and birthday presents you have saved up to £150 towards the cost of the horse, and your sister has emphasised that you will need £30 more than the purchase price to pay for a proper inspection of the horse by a vet.

HORSE OF THE YEAR
Briefing sheet

LEARNING
IN *ACTION*

Together with four of your friends you have decided to buy a horse or pony for your joint use. You have met to study the 'For Sale' columns of the *Horseman's Weekly* to decide which horse you will buy.

You know that two of your group have never ridden before, but you have helped out regularly for some months at the local riding stables and so are aware that for a youngster of your age a horse of more than 15.2 hands will be too big. You are also aware of the importance of a proper inspection by a vet before you complete your purchase as he is the best person to advise you whether it moves right. Your horse is going to require a stable or some other kind of shelter at least 3.75 metres square. You have £160 in a building society account as your share of the cost.

HORSE OF THE YEAR
Briefing sheet

Together with four of your friends you have decided to buy a horse or pony for your joint use. You have met to study the 'For Sale' columns of the *Horseman's Weekly* to decide which horse you will buy. . .

You have always been a regular saver and have £125 to go towards purchasing the horse. Your own riding experience is limited, but your father, a farmer who knows about these things, says that you should be able to get something reasonable for between £650 and £750..He has told you not to waste your money on a horse of 15 years or more; it may be cheaper, but there won't be much riding left in it. He will not allow you to get a stallion as this would be far too lively for youngsters of your age and lack of experience.

HORSE OF THE YEAR
Briefing sheet

Together with four of your friends you have decided to buy a horse or pony for your joint use. You have met to study the 'For Sale' columns of the *Horseman's Weekly* to decide which horse you will buy. . . .

You have never ridden before and are embarrassed as you have only £95 you can contribute to the cost of the horse, and no relatives who can afford to help you. What is more, you have heard people say that a 'good looker with a bit of Arab and thoroughbred' can cost up to £1000. However, your friends have told you not to worry as each of you is going to pay what you can manage. You have read an article in *Horse and Pony* and have found out that you need a horse at least 14.2 high, that mares are inadvisable for novices as they can be temperamental in season, and that before making a purchase you should enquire what the horse is like in traffic.

Together with four of your friends you have decided to buy a horse or pony for your joint use. You have met to study the 'For Sale' columns of the *Horseman's Weekly* to decide which horse you will buy. . . . .

You are one of the two in your group who has no experience of riding, so you have been on a pony trekking weekend with the Youth Club to find out what it is like. You have discovered that as a novice you must not have a horse with a difficult temperament. You enquired from your instructor about the cost of horses (with the help of your parents you can contribute £175) and she told you that you could probably pick up something for about £500, but that you could expect it to be cobby. It is worth paying rather more. She also emphasised how important it was to find out whether the horse was up to date with injections and worming.

E

RAWHIDE

Objective	• to improve individual and group problem-solving skills
Description	A problem-solving exercise set in the Wild West. Participants must devise a strategy to defeat Black Jake's evil intentions. There are both individual and group elements in this exercise which involves negotiating and influencing skills
Target group	Years 3–5
Organisation	Groups of 4–6 One tutor plus observers
Time required	1 hour
Tutor skill	B (see page 17)
Location	Plenary room plus group working areas with reasonable privacy
Materials	One briefing sheet per pupil

Tutor's notes

1. (Optional) Issue briefing sheet and allow individuals to work on the problem in their own time. (Ideal for homework or private study.)

2. The groups work on the problem. If individuals bring potential solutions with them, there may be a place for influencing and negotiating skills. (*20–45 minutes depending on ability of group and 1 above*)

3. *Review*
   Groups present their solutions and can be questioned by other groups and the tutor. Any dynamics within the group can also be discussed, and a list of problem-solving skills made. (*15–30 minutes*)

4. *Solution*
   Black Jake, travelling at 10 mph via Tombstone Valley, will reach Rawhide Ranch at 16.00 hours.

   Uncle Huck can reach Rawhide Ranch between 13.55 and 14.25 (depending on exactly when he is sent the message), but as he will not be able to persuade Katy-lou to leave and on his own can only delay two men (not four) for 15 minutes, he is really irrelevant.

   Some groups may treat Katy-lou as a 'man'. This is arguable in an age of equal rights, but it is unlikely that she is a 'man' when faced by the likes of Black Jake!

   Two men on horseback travelling by the secret path can be at the Ranch at 15.50 hours. They can then delay Black Jake's party long enough for the remainder of the group in the Steamcar, who can arrive at 16.12 if they travel via Redstone.

You are madly in love with Katy-lou, a beautiful young woman who lives at Rawhide Ranch, where she looks after her aged and bed-ridden grandfather.

At 12.00 hours you are alarmed at seeing Black Jake with three of his gang riding their mules at high speed through the town in the direction of Rawhide Ranch. Black Jake, proprietor of a disreputable bar in the town, is well-known for his evil intentions towards Katy-lou.

You immediately rush to the Sherriff's Office, where you find Sheriff Virgil Sippy and four of his men, prepared with you to form a posse to stop Black Jake. However, because of a serious outbreak of yellow equine fever, he only has two ancient horses available, which can only carry one man each and travel at 6 mph—in fact, Virgil says, after 20 miles they will drop dead.

The local transport manager is more helpful. He has available the very latest in cars, a superb Stanley Steam model, which can hold six people. It requires wood for fuel, carries enough for 50 miles and can develop a speed of 13 mph. Both horses and car can be ready by 12.30.

You think rapidly over the routes to Rawhide Ranch. There are three:

1 *By Tombstone Valley* 40 miles. This is a dangerous route, and it is extremely doubtful if a car can manage it, though there is plenty of firewood. Black Jake was seen heading this way.

2 *By Redstone* 48 miles. A good road, but no firewood.

3 *A Secret Path* Known only to yourself.
20 miles. Passable to mules and horses; impassable for a car.

Your mind switches to your Uncle Huck in Rotten Creek. Using the Sheriff's hand-signalling telegraph, you could get a message to him within 15 minutes. He lives on his own and has no transport, but he is only 5 miles from Rawhide Ranch and even in this rough countryside can manage 3 mph on foot.

For all practical purposes all men are equal in a fight, although one man should be able to delay two for 15 minutes. Similarly three should delay six for 15 minutes and so on.

Black Jake's mules were estimated to be travelling at 10 mph. Katy-lou will on no account desert her grandfather.

What are you going to do?

RESERVATIONS

Objective	• to improve joint problem-solving skills and cooperative group working
Description	Participants represent the organisers of a 6-a-side Hockey Championship and visiting school competitors. Each team's requirements need to be matched against a variety of hotel accommodation available in order to find a solution which satisfies them all
Target group	Years 3–5, 6th form
Organisation	Groups of 5–6 (4 school representatives 1 or 2 administrative assistants) One/two tutors plus observers
Time required	1¼ hours (minimum)
Tutor skill	C (see page 17)
Location	Any room in which groups can work with reasonable privacy
Materials	One briefing sheet for each member of the group (there are five sheets, all different) One *Accommodation List* for the Administrative Assistant(s)

Tutor's notes

1. Divide class into groups of 5–6. Distribute briefing sheets and *Accommodation Lists*. Allow a few minutes reading time. (*15 minutes*).

2. Groups work on the exercise (*35 minutes*)

3. Check answers and give solution (below) (*5 minutes*).

4. *Review*
   Points which should arise will include:
   • were the participants successful in solving the problem?
   • did they co-operate, or were they competitive (school *v* school, schools *v* administrative assistants)?
   • were basics established at the start—different schools; identities; nature of tournament . . ?
   • how was information shared?
   • who deliberately or incidentally helped or hindered the solution of the problem?
   (*20 minutes*)

5. *Solution*

Lauder College	Lee Arms
Talybont SFC	The Commuter
South Crayford School	Hotel Brennan: 7 double; 1 single; (bus and bar) Welcome Guest House: 6 double; 1 single (they are in the same street)
O'Driscoll Institute	Park Inn

   (It is tempting to put the O'Driscoll Institute in the Hotel Brennan as they are the only ones who can apparently afford it, but if this is done the others cannot be fitted in. The expense problem is tackled by linking the Hotel Brennan and Welcome Guest House, as detailed above, and pooling the costs.)

The United Kingdom Under 19 Indoor 6-a-side Hockey Championships are to be held in the Prince of Wales Stadium at Castleford. There are separate competitions for boys, girls and mixed teams.

As Administrative Assistant(s) to the Organiser, you have the responsibility for arranging accommodation for visiting schools. You are meeting with representatives of four of them: South Crayford School, Aldershot; Lauder College, Fife; Talybont SFC, Gwent; and The O'Driscoll Institute, Belfast, to finalise these arrangements. A list of available accommodation is attached, and the schools will each have their own requirements.

Your guidelines from the Organiser include the following:

1 The wishes of the competing schools should be met if at all possible.

2 Staff should have single rooms except where specifically requested otherwise.

3 Boys and girls must not share the same bedroom.

4 No pupils must be accommodated anywhere without a member of staff being present in the same hotel.

5 A mid-day meal is provided for all competitors and staff at the Stadium.

1 *Hotel Brennan* Russell Street

12 double, 2 single. Unlimited parking but one mile from nearest public transport. Vegetarian meals provided. Disco nightly. Bar. Swimming pool and squash court.

Tariff:
£21 per head per night for double room with half board
£23 per head per night for single room or for double room used by one person only. Half board.

2 *Park Inn* Boothgate

6 double, 4 single. Parking for private cars only, good public transport. Vegetarian meals provided. Bar. Close to municipal sports centre.

Tariff:
£20 per head per night for double room with half board.
£22 per head per night for single room or for double room used by one person only. Half board.

3 *Lee Arms* Station Road

10 double. Parking for private cars only, good public transport. No vegetarian meals. Disco and bar.

Tariff:
£16.50 per head per night with half board.

4 *The Commuter* Clogsole Lane

3 double, 3 single. Unlimited parking, good public transport. No vegetarian meals. No bar, but sauna.

Tariff:
£13.50 per head per night for double room with half board.
£14 per head per night for single room or for double room used by one person only. Half board.

5 *Welcome Guest House* Russell Street

6 double, 1 single. Parking for private cars only, no local bus route. BR station 2 miles. Unlicensed.

Tariff:
£9.50 per head per night, B & B
(A good hot set meal can be obtained at the nearby Haven Cafe for £2.50)

<table>
<tr><td>

RESERVATIONS
Lauder College, Fife

</td><td>

</td></tr>
</table>

You represent Lauder College, Fife. The College has entered two teams (one boys, one girls) for the United Kingdom Under 19 Indoor 6-a-side Hockey Championships to be held in the Prince of Wales Stadium at Castleford. You are meeting with the Administrative Assistant(s) to the Organiser to finalise accommodation.

Including reserves you will have seven boys and seven girls in your party. They will be accompanied by one male and one female member of staff, each of whom will require a single room. These members of staff will not be paying for their own accommodation, so sufficient funds will need to be available from the money paid by the pupils to cover their costs. You have told them they will need to provide £20 for bed, breakfast and evening meal, a mid-day meal being provided at the Stadium.

You are anxious that your hotel should have a disco or equivalent entertainment to keep your pupils occupied in the evenings.

<table>
<tr><td>

RESERVATIONS
Talybont SFC, Gwent

</td><td>

</td></tr>
</table>

You represent Talybont SFC, Gwent. The College has entered a mixed team for the United Kingdom Under 19 Indoor 6-a-side Hockey Championships to be held in the Prince of Wales Stadium at Castleford. You are meeting with the Administrative Assistant(s) to the Organiser to finalise accommodation.

Including one reserve you will have three boys and four girls in your party. They will be accompanied by one female and one male member of staff, each of whom will require a single room. The members of staff will be paying for their own accommodation. All members of your party have been told to allow £15 for bed, breakfast and evening meal, a mid-day meal being provided at the Stadium.

The College is an evangelical foundation with a long history of temperance, so you are insistent that your hotel should not contain a bar. As you are dependent on public transport, you need to be close to a bus route or the station.

RESERVATIONS
South Crayford School, Aldershot

You represent South Crayford School, Aldershot. The School has entered three teams (one girls, one boys, one mixed) for the United Kingdom Under 19 Indoor 6-a-side Hockey Championships to be held in the Prince of Wales Stadium at Castleford. You are meeting with the Administrative Assistant(s) to the Organiser to finalise accommodation.

Including reserves your party will have 12 girls and 12 boys. They will be accompanied by two female and two male members of staff; two are single and will require single rooms; the other two are a married couple. The members of staff will not be paying for their own accommodation, so sufficient funds will need to be available from the money paid by the pupils to cover their costs. You have told them they will need to provide £20 for bed, breakfast and evening meal, a mid-day meal being provided at the Stadium.

You will be travelling on the School bus and will require parking for it at your hotel. After unfortunate incidents in the evenings last year when several pupils went drinking in the town, you would like a bar in the hotel so that you can supervise their drinking activities.

RESERVATIONS
The O'Driscoll Institute, Belfast

You represent The O'Driscoll Institute in Belfast. The Institute has entered two girls teams for the United Kingdom Under 19 Indoor 6-a-side Hockey Championships to be held in the Prince of Wales Stadium at Castleford. You are meeting with the Administrative Assistant(s) to the Organiser to finalise accommodation.

Including one reserve you will have 13 girls in your party. They will be accompanied by one member of staff, who will require a single room but who will pay for her own accommodation. All members of your party have been told to allow £25 for bed, breakfast and evening meal, a mid-day meal being provided at the Stadium.

Several of the girls are vegetarian, so you definitely need a hotel providing vegetarian dishes. In addition the teams are very keen on keeping fit, and you would welcome a swimming pool, squash courts or other sporting facilities.

THE ARKBUCKLE BELL

Objective	• to improve joint problem-solving skills
Description	A problem-solving exercise in which participants have to deduce who has stolen the school's valuable bell. Each participant holds one vital clue, and only by sharing these can the culprit be identified
Target group	Years 4–5, CPVE students
Organisation	Groups of 5–7 One/two tutors (plus observers)
Time required	1 hour (minimum)
Tutor skill	C (see page 17)
Location	Any room in which groups can work with reasonable privacy
Materials	One briefing sheet per pupil (Sheets are in sets of five, all slightly different, but apparently the same. For the tutor's benefit they can be distinguished by the number of full stops at the end of the first paragraph ., .., ..., ..., ...) One *Form list* for each group

Tutor's notes

1. Form groups of 5–7. Distribute briefing sheets to each member of the group. If there are more than five, additional members can have a copy of any sheet. (*5 minutes*)

2. Groups work on the exercise (*30 minutes*)

3. Check answers. Discuss the solution (below). (*5 minutes*)

4. *Review*
   Groups should be encouraged to consider

   • organisation of the group: roles; leadership

   • sharing and display of essential information

   • arrangement of room for optimum working conditions

   • any relevant inter-personal behaviour

   (*20 minutes*)

5. *Solution*
   James Bland is the culprit. The others are exonerated as follows:

Raman Aziz	Not fair hair	Alibi		Denims
Winston Clyde	Not fair hair	Alibi		
Butch Johson	Not fair hair			
Samson S Jones	Not fair hair			
Ged Norobov				Denims
Bob Simpson		Alibi		
Argyle Smith	Not fair hair	Alibi		
Titch Smith			Height	
Curly Winston		Alibi	Height	

Bricktown School is situated in the town centre of Chumleigh Episcopi. Chumleigh was 200 years ago an attractive market town, the centre of the local agricultural community and the seat of the Bishop of Leyland. However, the discovery of coal some 150 years ago, combined with the growth of a prosperous tin-plate industry in the early years of this century, radically altered the nature both of the town and the community. The graceful medieval buildings were pulled down to conform to the needs of the new industry, and hundreds of terraced houses for the workforce mushroomed in the area. By 1926 the town had grown to accommodate 30 000 people and was a thriving industrial and commercial centre. Fortunes changed in the '30s when the area was badly hit by the depression. Enemy bombing in the war, the exhaustion of the mines and the collapse of the tin-plate industry added to the decline of the town. It is now run-down and shabby, with areas of inner-city dereliction. Unemployment runs at about 20% and the crime rate is high.

Bricktown School's prize possession is the Arkbuckle Bell which has the place of honour in the school's entrance hall. It was presented in memory of the school's most famous old student, Cdr Quintin Arkbuckle DSO, and is in fact the ship's bell of HMS Swordfish of which Cdr Arkbuckle was captain at the time of his death in action off Sumatra in 1943.

The bell has considerable sentimental and some commercial value. The local Crime Prevention Officer recommended that it should be locked away and no longer left in its position of prominence in the entrance hall where it could be so easily stolen or damaged. But the Headmistress has firmly refused to consider this.

On the evening of June 15th the bell was stolen. It had been seen in its normal place by the Headmistress when she left the school at 8.00 pm, but was missing when the caretaker went on his rounds to lock up at 10.00 pm. The theft was immediately reported to the police, and a request for information was made at Assembly next morning.

As a result of this request, a girl in the 1st Year, Wendy Gill, went to see the headmistress. She said that she had been walking her dog across the playground soon after 9.00 pm, when a boy ran out of the school carrying the bell. She did not know the boy, nor could she give a description, other than he was wearing trainers and denims and was of medium height, but she thought that he was 'one of that gang in 4Z'.

4Z is one of the problem forms in the school. It is predominantly made up of boys, few with any great academic ability and mainly from the most depressed area of the town. Several have been in trouble with the police for a variety of offences. For instance, Bob Simpson and Argyle Smith are on probation for stealing milk bottles off doorsteps. Titch Smith was recently involved in a fight outside the Black Swan, his father's pub. Curly Winslow has convictions in the juvenile court for riding an uninsured and unlicensed motor cycle on the public highway while still under age. And Butch Johnson was suspected of breaking and entering the local branch of the Co-op, though this was never proved.

The class, however, has been a positive menace in school. Few staff enjoy teaching it because of the low standard of discipline and poor attitude to school work. The boys are frequently found to be misbehaving in stupid ways about the school—talking in assembly, smoking in the toilets, baiting the dinner ladies. And it is suspected that they have been running a local extortion racket, demanding protection money from younger pupils. In an otherwise well-disciplined school with a high reputation in the community they represent a rare but serious challenge to authority and to the school's good name.

Immediately the Headmistress had received Wendy Gill's information, the police were summoned and provided with a list of all the boys in 4Z. This list is attached. Each boy was interviewed in turn, but all denied knowledge of the offence. When asked to give an account of their movements between 8 and 10 pm the previous evening, most were unable to do so, but Winston Clyde and Argyle Smith claimed to have been at the Western Street Youth Centre Disco; Raman Aziz visiting his grandmother in South Street; and Curly Winslow at an ACF Parade at the TA Centre in Fortress Road. All these alibis were checked and found to be correct. The police examined their clothing and found that all of them regularly wore trainers and denims.

The incident created considerable interest in the town and information continued to reach the police. All of this was subsequently checked and found to be true, but much seemed to have little relevance. A bell similar to the Arkbuckle Bell had been offered to a second-hand dealer in Beggars Row; lights had been reported burning at the school at 11.00 pm; a boy had been seen carrying the bell at about 9.20 pm; a phone call had been received by the Headmistress at 9.30 pm—a boy's voice claimed with a wealth of foul language that the bell had been stolen and that he knew who had taken it, but she had dismissed this simply as a rare example of an abusive anonymous phone call.

Who had stolen the Arkbuckle Bell?

Bricktown School is situated in the town centre of Chumleigh Episcopi. Chumleigh was 200 years ago an attractive market town, the centre of the local agricultural community and the seat of the Bishop of Leyland. However, the discovery of coal some 150 years ago, combined with the growth of a prosperous tin-plate industry in the early years of this century, radically altered the nature both of the town and the community. The graceful medieval buildings were pulled down to conform to the needs of the new industry, and hundreds of terraced houses for the workforce mushroomed in the area. By 1926 the town had grown to accommodate 30 000 people and was a thriving industrial and commercial centre. Fortunes changed in the '30s when the area was badly hit by the depression. Enemy bombing in the war, the exhaustion of the mines and the collapse of the tin-plate industry added to the decline of the town. It is now run-down and shabby, with areas of inner-city dereliction. Unemployment runs at about 20% and the crime rate is high..

Bricktown School's prize possession is the Arkbuckle Bell which has the place of honour in the school's entrance hall. It was presented in memory of the school's most famous old student, Cdr Quintin Arkbuckle DSO, and is in fact the ship's bell of HMS Swordfish of which Cdr Arkbuckle was captain at the time of his death in action off Sumatra in 1943.

The bell has considerable sentimental and some commercial value. The local Crime Prevention Officer recommended that it should be locked away and no longer left in its position of prominence in the entrance hall where it could be so easily stolen or damaged. But the Headmistress has firmly refused to consider this.

On the evening of June 15th the bell was stolen. It had been seen in its normal place by the Headmistress when she left the school at 8.00 pm, but was missing when the caretaker went on his rounds to lock up at 10.00 pm. The theft was immediately reported to the police, and a request for information was made at Assembly next morning.

As a result of this request, a girl in the 1st Year, Wendy Gill, went to see the Headmistress. She said that she had been walking her dog across the playground soon after 9.00 pm, when a boy ran out of the school carrying the bell. She did not know the boy, nor could she give a description, other than he was wearing trainers and denims and had fair hair, but she thought that he was 'one of that gang in 4Z'.

4Z is one of the problem forms in the school. It is predominantly made up of boys, few with any great academic ability and mainly from the most depressed area of the town. Several have been in trouble with the police for a variety of offences. For instance, Bob Simpson and Argyle Smith are on probation for stealing milk bottles off doorsteps. Titch Smith was recently involved in a fight outside the Black Swan, his father's pub. Curly Winslow has convictions in the juvenile court for riding an uninsured and unlicensed motor cycle on the public highway while still under age. And Butch Johnson was suspected of breaking and entering the local branch of the Co-op, though this was never proved.

The class, however, has been a positive menace in school. Few staff enjoy teaching it because of the low standard of discipline and poor attitude to school work. The boys are frequently found to be misbehaving in stupid ways about the school—talking in assembly, smoking in the toilets, baiting the dinner ladies. And it is suspected that they have been running a local extortion racket, demanding protection money from younger pupils. In an otherwise well-disciplined school with a high reputation in the community they represent a rare but serious challenge to authority and to the school's good name.

Immediately the Headmistress had received Wendy Gill's information, the police were summoned and provided with a list of all the boys in 4Z. This list is attached. Each boy was interviewed in turn, but all denied knowledge of the offence. When asked to give an account of their movements between 8 and 10 pm the previous evening, most were unable to do so, but Winston Clyde and Argyie Smith claimed to have been at the Western Street Youth Centre Disco; Raman Aziz visiting his grandmother in South Street; and Curly Winslow at an ACF Parade at the TA Centre in Fortress Road. All these alibis were checked and found to be correct. The police examined their clothing and found that all of them regularly wore trainers and denims.

The incident created considerable interest in the town and information continued to reach the police. All of this was subsequently checked and found to be true, but much seemed to have little relevance. A bell similar to the Arkbuckle Bell had been offered to a second-hand dealer in Beggars Row; lights had been reported burning at the school at 11.00 pm; a boy had been seen carrying the bell at about 9.20 pm; a phone call had been received by the Headmistress at 9.30 pm—a boy's voice claimed with a wealth of foul language that the bell had been stolen and that he knew who had taken it, but she had dismissed this simply as a rare example of an abusive anonymous phone call.

Who had stolen the Arkbuckle Bell?

Bricktown School is situated in the town centre of Chumleigh Episcopi. Chumleigh was 200 years ago an attractive market town, the centre of the local agricultural community and the seat of the Bishop of Leyland. However, the discovery of coal some 150 years ago, combined with the growth of a prosperous tin-plate industry in the early years of this century, radically altered the nature both of the town and the community. The graceful medieval buildings were pulled down to conform to the needs of the new industry, and hundreds of terraced houses for the workforce mushroomed in the area. By 1926 the town had grown to accommodate 30 000 people and was a thriving industrial and commercial centre. Fortunes changed in the '30s when the area was badly hit by the depression. Enemy bombing in the war, the exhaustion of the mines and the collapse of the tin-plate industry added to the decline of the town. It is now run-down and shabby, with areas of inner-city dereliction. Unemployment runs at about 20% and the crime rate is high...

Bricktown School's prize possession is the Arkbuckle Bell which has the place of honour in the school's entrance hall. It was presented in memory of the school's most famous old student, Cdr Quintin Arkbuckle DSO, and is in fact the ship's bell of HMS Swordfish of which Cdr Arkbuckle was captain at the time of his death in action off Sumatra in 1943.

The bell has considerable sentimental and some commercial value. The local Crime Prevention Officer recommended that it should be locked away and no longer left in its position of prominence in the entrance hall where it could be so easily stolen or damaged. But the Headmistress has firmly refused to consider this.

On the evening of June 15th the bell was stolen. It had been seen in its normal place by the Headmistress when she left the school at 8.00 pm, but was missing when the caretaker went on his rounds to lock up at 10.00 pm. The theft was immediately reported to the police, and a request for information was made at Assembly next morning.

As a result of this request, a girl in the 1st Year, Wendy Gill, went to see the Headmistress. She said that she had been walking her dog across the playground soon after 9.00 pm, when a boy ran out of the school carrying the bell. She did not know the boy, nor could she give a description, other than he was wearing trainers and denims, but she thought that he was 'one of that gang in 4Z'.

4Z is one of the problem forms in the school. It is predominantly made up of boys, few with any great academic ability and mainly from the most depressed area of the town. Several have been in trouble with the police for a variety of offences. For instance, Bob Simpson and Argyle Smith are on probation for stealing milk bottles off doorsteps. Titch Smith was recently involved in a fight outside the Black Swan, his father's pub. Curly Winslow has convictions in the juvenile court for riding an uninsured and unlicensed motor cycle on the public highway while still under age. And Butch Johnson was suspected of breaking and entering the local branch of the Co-op, though this was never proved.

The class, however, has been a positive menace in school. Few staff enjoy teaching it because of the low standard of discipline and poor attitude to school work. The boys are frequently found to be misbehaving in stupid ways about the school—talking in assembly, smoking in the toilets, baiting the dinner ladies. And it is suspected that they have been running a local extortion racket, demanding protection money from younger pupils. In an otherwise well-disciplined school with a high reputation in the community they represent a rare but serious challenge to authority and to the school's good name.

Immediately the Headmistress had received Wendy Gill's information, the police were summoned and provided with a list of all the boys in 4Z. This list is attached. Each boy was interviewed in turn, but all denied knowledge of the offence. When asked to give an account of their movements between 8 and 10 pm the previous evening, most were unable to do so, but Winston Clyde, Bob Simpson and Argyle Smith claimed to have been at the Western Street Youth Centre Disco; Raman Aziz visiting his grandmother in South Street; and Curly Winslow at an ACF Parade at the TA Centre in Fortress Road. All these alibis were checked and found to be correct. The police examined their clothing and found that all of them regularly wore trainers and denims.

The incident created considerable interest in the town and information continued to reach the police. All of this was subsequently checked and found to be true, but much seemed to have little relevance. A bell similar to the Arkbuckle Bell had been offered to a second-hand dealer in Beggars Row; lights had been reported burning at the school at 11.00 pm; a boy had been seen carrying the bell at about 9.20 pm; a phone call had been received by the Headmistress at 9.30 pm—a boy's voice claimed with a wealth of foul language that the bell had been stolen and that he knew who had taken it, but she had dismissed this simply as a rare example of an abusive anonymous phone call.

Who had stolen the Arkbuckle Bell?

LEARNING
IN *ACTION*

Bricktown School is situated in the town centre of Chumleigh Episcopi. Chumleigh was 200 years ago an attractive market town, the centre of the local agricultural community and the seat of the Bishop of Leyland. However, the discovery of coal some 150 years ago, combined with the growth of a prosperous tin-plate industry in the early years of this century, radically altered the nature both of the town and the community. The graceful medieval buildings were pulled down to conform to the needs of the new industry, and hundreds of terraced houses for the workforce mushroomed in the area. By 1926 the town had grown to accommodate 30 000 people and was a thriving industrial and commercial centre. Fortunes changed in the '30s when the area was badly hit by the depression. Enemy bombing in the war, the exhaustion of the mines and the collapse of the tin-plate industry added to the decline of the town. It is now run-down and shabby, with areas of inner-city dereliction. Unemployment runs at about 20% and the crime rate is high....

Bricktown School's prize possession is the Arkbuckle Bell which has the place of honour in the school's entrance hall. It was presented in memory of the school's most famous old student, Cdr Quintin Arkbuckle DSO, and is in fact the ship's bell of HMS Swordfish of which Cdr Arkbuckle was captain at the time of his death in action off Sumatra in 1943.

The bell has considerable sentimental and some commercial value. The local Crime Prevention Officer recommended that it should be locked away and no longer left in its position of prominence in the entrance hall where it could be so easily stolen or damaged. But the Headmistress has firmly refused to consider this.

On the evening of June 15th the bell was stolen. It had been seen in its normal place by the Headmistress when she left the school at 8.00 pm, but was missing when the caretaker went on his rounds to lock up at 10.00 pm. The theft was immediately reported to the police, and a request for information was made at Assembly next morning.

As a result of this request, a girl in the 1st Year, Wendy Gill, went to see the Headmistress. She said that she had been walking her dog across the playground soon after 9.00 pm, when a boy ran out of the school carrying the bell. She did not know the boy, nor could she give a description, other than he was wearing trainers and denims, but she thought that he was 'one of that gang in 4Z'.

4Z is one of the problem forms in the school. It is predominantly made up of boys, few with any great academic ability and mainly from the most depressed area of the town. Several have been in trouble with the police for a variety of offences. For instance, Bob Simpson and Argyle Smith are on probation for stealing milk bottles off doorsteps. Titch Smith was recently involved in a fight outside the Black Swan, his father's pub. Curly Winslow has convictions in the juvenile court for riding an uninsured and unlicensed motor cycle on the public highway while still under age. And Butch Johnson was suspected of breaking and entering the local branch of the Co-op, though this was never proved.

The class, however, has been a positive menace in school. Few staff enjoy teaching it because of the low standard of discipline and poor attitude to school work. The boys are frequently found to be misbehaving in stupid ways about the school—talking in assembly, smoking in the toilets, baiting the dinner ladies. And it is suspected that they have been running a local extortion racket, demanding protection money from younger pupils. In an otherwise well-disciplined school with a high reputation in the community they represent a rare but serious challenge to authority and to the school's good name.

Immediately the Headmistress had received Wendy Gill's information, the police were summoned and provided with a list of all the boys in 4Z. This list is attached. Each boy was interviewed in turn, but all denied knowledge of the offence. When asked to give an account of their movements between 8 and 10 pm the previous evening, most were unable to do so, but Winston Clyde and Argyle Smith claimed to have been at the Western Street Youth Centre Disco; Raman Aziz visiting his grandmother in South Street; and Curly Winslow at an ACF Parade at the TA Centre in Fortress Road. All these alibis were checked and found to be correct. The police examined their clothing and found that all of them regularly wore trainers and denims though Raman Aziz's were unusable because they were ripped.

The incident created considerable interest in the town and information continued to reach the police. All of this was subsequently checked and found to be true, but much seemed to have little relevance. A bell similar to the Arkbuckle Bell had been offered to a second-hand dealer in Beggars Row; lights had been reported burning at the school at 11.00 pm; a boy had been seen carrying the bell at about 9.20 pm; a phone call had been received by the Headmistress at 9.30 pm—a boy's voice claimed with a wealth of foul language that the bell had been stolen and that he knew who had taken it, but she had dismissed this simply as a rare example of an abusive anonymous phone call.

Who had stolen the Arkbuckle Bell?

Bricktown School is situated in the town centre of Chumleigh Episcopi. Chumleigh was 200 years ago an attractive market town, the centre of the local agricultural community and the seat of the Bishop of Leyland. However, the discovery of coal some 150 years ago, combined with the growth of a prosperous tin-plate industry in the early years of this century, radically altered the nature both of the town and the community. The graceful medieval buildings were pulled down to conform to the needs of the new industry, and hundreds of terraced houses for the workforce mushroomed in the area. By 1926 the town had grown to accommodate 30 000 people and was a thriving industrial and commercial centre. Fortunes changed in the '30s when the area was badly hit by the depression. Enemy bombing in the war, the exhaustion of the mines and the collapse of the tin-plate industry added to the decline of the town. It is now run-down and shabby, with areas of inner-city dereliction. Unemployment runs at about 20% and the crime rate is high.....

Bricktown School's prize possession is the Arkbuckle Bell which has the place of honour in the school's entrance hall. It was presented in memory of the school's most famous old student, Cdr Quintin Arkbuckle DSO, and is in fact the ship's bell of HMS Swordfish of which Cdr Arkbuckle was captain at the time of his death in action off Sumatra in 1943.

The bell has considerable sentimental and some commercial value. The local Crime Prevention Officer recommended that it should be locked away and no longer left in its position of prominence in the entrance hall where it could be so easily stolen or damaged. But the Headmistress has firmly refused to consider this.

On the evening of June 15th the bell was stolen. It had been seen in its normal place by the Headmistress when she left the school at 8.00 pm, but was missing when the caretaker went on his rounds to lock up at 10.00 pm. The theft was immediately reported to the police, and a request for information was made at Assembly next morning.

As a result of this request, a girl in the 1st Year, Wendy Gill, went to see the Headmistress. She said that she had been walking her dog across the playground soon after 9.00 pm, when a boy ran out of the school carrying the bell. She did not know the boy, nor could she give a description, other than he was wearing trainers and denims, but she thought that he was 'one of that gang in 4Z'.

4Z is one of the problem forms in the school. It is predominantly made up of boys, few with any great academic ability and mainly from the most depressed area of the town. Several have been in trouble with the police for a variety of offences. For instance, Bob Simpson and Argyle Smith are on probation for stealing milk bottles off doorsteps. Titch Smith was recently involved in a fight outside the Black Swan, his father's pub. Curly Winslow has convictions in the juvenile court for riding an uninsured and unlicensed motor cycle on the public highway while still under age. And Butch Johnson was suspected of breaking and entering the local branch of the Co-op, though this was never proved.

The class, however, has been a positive menace in school. Few staff enjoy teaching it because of the low standard of discipline and poor attitude to school work. The boys are frequently found to be misbehaving in stupid ways about the school—talking in assembly, smoking in the toilets, baiting the dinner ladies. And it is suspected that they have been running a local extortion racket, demanding protection money from younger pupils. In an otherwise well-disciplined school with a high reputation in the community they represent a rare but serious challenge to authority and to the school's good name.

Immediately the Headmistress had received Wendy Gill's information, the police were summoned and provided with a list of all the boys in 4Z. This list is attached. Each boy was interviewed in turn, but all denied knowledge of the offence. When asked to give an account of their movements between 8 and 10 pm the previous evening, most were unable to do so, but Winston Clyde and Argyle Smith claimed to have been at the Western Street Youth Centre Disco; Raman Aziz visiting his grandmother in South Street; and Curly Winslow at an ACF Parade at the TA Centre in Fortress Road. All these alibis were checked and found to be correct. The police examined their clothing and found that all of them regularly wore trainers and denims though Ged Norobov's had been in the wash for two days.

The incident created considerable interest in the town and information continued to reach the police. All of this was subsequently checked and found to be true, but much seemed to have little relevance. A bell similar to the Arkbuckle Bell had been offered to a second-hand dealer in Beggars Row; lights had been reported burning at the school at 11.00 pm; a boy had been seen carrying the bell at about 9.20 pm; a phone call had been received by the Headmistress at 9.30 pm—a boy's voice claimed with a wealth of foul language that the bell had been stolen and that he knew who had taken it, but she had dismissed this simply as a rare example of an abusive anonymous phone call.

Who had stolen the Arkbuckle Bell?

THE ARKBUCKLE BELL
Form list

LEARNING IN *ACTION*

Form 4Z   **Boys**

NAME	AGE	ADDRESS	HEIGHT	COLOUR
AZIZ, Raman	14:9	17 Norbury Close	174 cm	Coloured
BLAND, James	14:11	24 Western St.	166 cm	White
CLYDE, Winston	15:5	75 Western St.	176 cm	Black
JOHNSON, Butch	15:0	3 Norbury Close	172 cm	Black
JONES, Samson S.	15:2	6 West Way	177 cm	Black
NOROBOV, Ged	14:9	17 Wentworth St.	164 cm	White
SIMPSON, Bob	15:4	76 Western St.	169 cm	White
SMITH, Argyle	15:4	15 Western St.	170 cm	Black
SMITH, Titch	15:2	The Black Swan, North Street	190 cm	White
WINSLOW, Curly	15:8	48 Newport Way	153 cm	White

CAPITATION COMMITTEE

Objective	• to improve negotiating, influencing and consensus skills
Description	As the title implies, this problem explores the allocation of funds within a school. Participants represent individual departments and are required to negotiate a satisfactory solution
Target group	Staff, possibly 6th form
Organisation	Groups of 5 One/two tutors plus observers
Time required	1¼ hours
Tutor skill	B (see page 17)
Location	Any room in which groups can work with reasonable privacy
Materials	One briefing sheet per participant (Sheets are in sets of five, all different)

Tutor's notes

1. Distribute briefing sheets. Allow five minutes for participants to plan their courses of action. (*10 minutes*)

2. Groups work on problem (*35–45 minutes*)

3. *Review*
   Points which should emerge will include:
   - how did the group organise itself?
   - how was the money distributed?
   - what factors influenced the group's decision?
   - who influenced whom? How?
   - how did individuals cope when they were asked for information that was not in the briefing sheets?
   - any relevant inter-personal behaviour

   (*30 minutes*)

You are a member of the Capitation Committee of Swan Upper School. The School receives £35 000 in capitation, and of this £2500 is set aside to provide additional resources to assist Departments which are involved in curriculum development, such as the introduction of new courses, or which have special needs. You have met to allocate this money.

You represent the English Department which this year has a particular problem brought about by the introduction of new examination set texts. At 'A' level, for instance, where you expect about 15 students, you have to buy copies of Chaucer and Coleridge, *King Lear* and *Othello*, *The Return of the Native* and *Catch 22*. Even by using paperbacks where available, the total cost will be £555.95. GCSE level texts, where there are fewer changes, will cost a further £125.50.

The total capitation of the Department is only £2218 which is comfortably taken up by texts for general study throughout the school, course books and stationery.

The English Department consistently has some of the best examination results in the school, yet during a recent visit of HMI adverse comment was expressed about the age and condition of many of the books in regular use.

CAPITATION COMMITTEE
Briefing sheet: Language Department

LEARNING
IN *ACTION*

You are a member of the Capitation Committee of Swan Upper School. The School receives £35 000 in capitation, and of this £2500 is set aside to provide additional resources to assist Departments which are involved in curriculum development, such as the introduction of new courses, or which have special needs. You have met to allocate this money.

You represent the Languages Department whose normal capitation is £1402. The Department has a new Head who is busy introducing a foreign language to a wider cross-section of the school, at the same time as adopting new examination syllabi in both French and German. This will involve new text books in the 4th Year which certainly cannot be provided from normal capitation. A set of *Kapiert 2* with teacher's book will cost £162.25; *Tricolore 4* is more expensive (£714.45), as it includes two pupils' books and also films and tapes.

With these new courses you anticipate a growth of interest in languages among the pupils and a consequent improvement in examination results.

CAPITATION COMMITTEE
Briefing sheet: Business Studies Department

LEARNING
IN *ACTION*

You are a member of the Capitation Committee of Swan Upper School. The School receives £35 000 in capitation, and of this £2500 is set aside to provide additional resources to assist Departments which are involved in curriculum development, such as the introduction of new courses, or which have special needs. You have met to allocate this money.

You represent the Business Studies Department. As you only teach pupils in the 4th, 5th and 6th Forms, your capitation is a mere £899. Your Department was set up 15 years ago with 40 new typewriters. Since then it has only been possible to purchase three manual and two electronic machines, so the condition of the remainder is decidedly poor. In any case, with the introduction of CPVE and many pupils looking for careers as secretaries or in information technology, you feel it is important for the Department to be stocked with up-to-date equipment. Each new electronic machine costs £300; it would cost £6000 to completely re-equip a room.

CAPITATION COMMITTEE
Briefing sheet: CDT Department

You are a member of the Capitation Committee of Swan Upper School. The School receives £35 000 in capitation, and of this £2500 is set aside to provide additional resources to assist Departments which are involved in curriculum development, such as the introduction of new courses, or which have special needs. You have met to allocate this money.

You represent the Craft, Design and Technology Department, which is anxious to introduce Control Technology as a new course. You consider it most important to do this in order that pupils may benefit from the latest aspects of the technological curriculum and that the school may be seen to be abreast of curricular development. As your existing capitation is already fully committed, Control Technology can only be provided if extra resources are available. The initial 'kit' can be obtained for the next three months at a bargain rate of £1026, and a further £200 will be needed for other items. You have been offered £500 towards this from a private charitable trust, provided the School produces the remainder of the money.

CAPITATION COMMITTEE
Briefing sheet: Science Department

You are a member of the Capitation Committee of Swan Upper School. The School receives £35 000 in capitation, and of this £2500 is set aside to provide additional resources to assist Departments which are involved in curriculum development, such as the introduction of new courses, or which have special needs. You have met to allocate this money.

You represent the Science Department, which has been placed in extreme financial difficulty by the rise in the prices of chemicals and glassware over the past two years. In that time ignition tubes have risen by 27.8%, test tubes by 20.8% and methanol by 28.6%. Potassium bromide and benedict's solution have risen by 43% and 69% respectively over the past 18 months; and sodium nitrate and glucose by 48% and 13.3% in the past year. Despite spending over £519 on glassware and chemicals last year, you ran out of stock. This year you estimate that these items will cost not less than £700, and that sum simply cannot be found out of your capitation of £3654.

HOLIDAY ROTA

Objective	• to improve negotiating skills
Description	A common group problem—how a holiday rota can be arranged—which may be either a negotiation or a consensus exercise, depending upon the group.
Target group	Years 4, 5 and 6th form
Organisation	Groups of 5 One tutor plus observers
Time required	1¼ hours
Tutor skill	B (see page 17)
Location	Any room in which groups can work with reasonable privacy
Materials	One briefing sheet (sheets are in sets of five, all different) and one rota calendar per participant

Tutor's notes

1. Divide the class into groups of 5. Issue each participant with briefing sheet and rota calendar. (*5 minutes*)

2. Reading and planning time. (*10 minutes*)

3. Negotiation (*30 minutes*)

4. Examine results and identify the most 'successful' negotiators (*5 minutes*)

3. *Review*
   There is no 'best answer' to this negotiation. Participants can get three first choices or three third choices according to their negotiating skill. Points that should emerge will include:

   a Principles of negotiation
   - what skills are needed to negotiate successfully by individuals and by groups?
   - what skills were present or missing on this occasion?

   b The negotiation itself
   How did the participants
   - reconcile 'a convenient rota' with 'personal success'? Were they co-operative or competitive?
   - plan their tactics and use the rota calendar? Were they flexible?
   - view special cases eg the marriage, the county championships?
   - cope with particular problems eg did the two who needed to be on holiday at the same time for the wedding ignore the problem, ask special permission from the Company (tutor), or give up?
     Did the participants realise there was no third choice date here?
   - cope with the time factor?

   (*25 minutes*)

You work for Wrightbite Confectionery Ltd, an old-established firm of chocolate manufacturers. Mr Wright, the Chairman, likes his employees to have the opportunity of choosing their holiday dates where possible, but because of the size of the firm (only 50 employees) and the seasonal nature of quality chocolate production, the choice cannot be totally free.

Younger employees, of whom you are one, are entitled to four weeks holiday a year, one of which must be taken between Christmas and New Year. The autumn and spring are dominated by the seasonal demands of the Christmas novelty and Easter egg trade, so the remaining three weeks holiday must be taken during the months of May, June, July and August. Mr Wright is happy for you younger ones to arrange your own holiday rota, with the proviso that he can only allow one of you to be away at any one time.

You are engaged to be married and the wedding has been arranged for May 11th. Your first choice of dates is therefore the fortnight beginning on that day. You would like your closest friend who also works at Wrightbite, to be free at that time as well to assist at the ceremony. If that fortnight were out of the question, it would just about be possible to arrange the wedding on July 13th, with the honeymoon during the period July 13th–27th, but this would be very unpopular with your in-laws. For your other week, your first choice would be that beginning on August 24th, second choice August 17th and third August 10th. You do not wish to be away during the Town Gala which lasts for the fortnight from June 29th to July 13th.

Your task is to negotiate with your colleagues to arrange a rota agreed by and convenient to all of you. This rota should be recorded on the form provided and handed to your tutor. You have 30 minutes to complete this task, otherwise your holidays will be arranged for you.

You can estimate your personal success by scoring 10 points for every one of your first choice weeks which is included in the rota, 6 points for a second choice, 3 points for a third choice, and 0 points if you accept a week you had not requested at all.

© 1987   Roger Kirk   Basil Blackwell

HOLIDAY ROTA
Employee 2

LEARNING
IN *ACTION*

You work for Wrightbite Confectionery Ltd, an old-established firm of chocolate manufacturers. Mr Wright, the Chairman, likes his employees to have the opportunity of choosing their holiday dates where possible, but because of the size of the firm (only 50 employees) and the seasonal nature of quality chocolate production, the choice cannot be totally free.

Younger employees, of whom you are one, are entitled to four weeks holiday a year, one of which must be taken between Christmas and New Year. The autumn and spring are dominated by the seasonal demands of the Christmas novelty and Easter egg trade, so the remaining three weeks holiday must be taken during the months of May, June, July and August. Mr Wright is happy for you younger ones to arrange your own holiday rota, with the proviso that he can only allow one of you to be away at any one time.

You are a keen cricket enthusiast and would like to take the three individual weeks which coincide with the county team playing on the local ground. These weeks are those beginning on May 11th, July 27th and August 24th. Your second choices are the weeks beginning May 25th, June 22nd and August 3rd when the team is playing elsewhere in the county. Otherwise you will be forced to travel to out-of-county matches which is expensive and inconvenient. However, if all else fails you would be prepared to accept the weeks beginning May 4th, July 13th and August 17th.

On no account do you wish to be away between June 29th and July 13th. This is the Town Gala when there is much local cricket activity in the evenings and at week-ends.

Your task is to negotiate with your colleagues to arrange a rota agreed by and convenient to all of you. This rota should be recorded on the form provided and handed to your tutor. You have 30 minutes to complete this task, otherwise your holidays will be arranged for you.

You can estimate your personal success by scoring 10 points for every one of your first choice weeks which is included in the rota, 6 points for a second choice, 3 points for a third choice, and 0 points if you accept a week you had not requested at all.

You work for Wrightbite Confectionery Ltd, an old-established firm of chocolate manufacturers. Mr Wright, the Chairman, likes his employees to have the opportunity of choosing their holiday dates where possible, but because of the size of the firm (only 50 employees) and the seasonal nature of quality chocolate production, the choice cannot be totally free.

Younger employees, of whom you are one, are entitled to four weeks holiday a year, one of which must be taken between Christmas and New Year. The autumn and spring are dominated by the seasonal demands of the Christmas novelty and Easter egg trade, so the remaining three weeks holiday must be taken during the months of May, June, July and August. Mr Wright is happy for you younger ones to arrange your own holiday rota, with the proviso that he can only allow one of you to be away at any one time.

You have the opportunity of going with friends on a walking holiday in Scotland. This will take three weeks, and the dates arranged are the period beginning May 25th. You have told your friends that you do not have a completely free choice of dates, and they could manage as a reluctant second best the three weeks starting on July 27th, but this would be far less convenient. Failing this you would have to go walking on your own, which is certainly a third choice option. You would then choose the three weeks starting May 4th.

Whatever happens you do not want to be away from home during the Town Gala (June 29th–July 12th incl) as that is always the occasion of a family get-together.

Your task is to negotiate with your colleagues to arrange a rota agreed by and convenient to all of you. This rota should be recorded on the form provided and handed to your tutor. You have 30 minutes to complete this task, otherwise your holidays will be arranged for you.

You can estimate your personal success by scoring 10 points for every one of your first choice weeks which is included in the rota, 6 points for a second choice, 3 points for a third choice, and 0 points if you accept a week you had not requested at all.

HOLIDAY ROTA
Employee 4

You work for Wrightbite Confectionery Ltd, an old-established firm of chocolate manufacturers. Mr Wright, the Chairman, likes his employees to have the opportunity of choosing their holiday dates where possible, but because of the size of the firm (only 50 employees) and the seasonal nature of quality chocolate production, the choice cannot be totally free.

Younger employees, of whom you are one, are entitled to four weeks holiday a year, one of which must be taken between Christmas and New Year. The autumn and spring are dominated by the seasonal demands of the Christmas novelty and Easter egg trade, so the remaining three weeks holiday must be taken during the months of May, June, July and August. Mr Wright is happy for you younger ones to arrange your own holiday rota, with the proviso that he can only allow one of you to be away at any one time.

This year you are looking forward to a three-week coach tour of Switzerland and Austria with your fiancé(e) who has never been abroad before. Tours depart weekly, and easily the most convenient for both of you is the one which leaves on July 13th. As coaches get very booked up, you have been asked to nominate alternative dates, and you have given as your second choice the three weeks starting on August 10th, and as your third choice the tour leaving on June 8th. Your fiancé(e)'s job as Personal Assistant to the Town's Recreation Manager means that other dates are extremely difficult, while the fortnight of the Town Gala (June 29th–July 13th) is out of the question.

Your task is to negotiate with your colleagues to arrange a rota agreed by and convenient to all of you. This rota should be recorded on the form provided and handed to your tutor. You have 30 minutes to complete this task, otherwise your holidays will be arranged for you.

You can estimate your personal success by scoring 10 points for every one of your first choice weeks which is included in the rota, 6 points for a second choice, 3 points for a third choice, and 0 points if you accept a week you had not requested at all.

HOLIDAY ROTA
Employee 5

You work for Wrightbite Confectionery Ltd, an old-established firm of chocolate manufacturers. Mr Wright, the Chairman, likes his employees to have the opportunity of choosing their holiday dates where possible, but because of the size of the firm (only 50 employees) and the seasonal nature of quality chocolate production, the choice cannot be totally free.

Younger employees, of whom you are one, are entitled to four weeks holiday a year, one of which must be taken between Christmas and New Year. The autumn and spring are dominated by the seasonal demands of the Christmas novelty and Easter egg trade, so the remaining three weeks holiday must be taken during the months of May, June, July and August. Mr Wright is happy for you younger ones to arrange your own holiday rota, with the proviso that he can only allow one of you to be away at any one time.

The first priority for your holiday is to assist at the wedding on May 11th of your best friend who also works for the company. This means that you would like to take the week starting on that date. Your friend has told you that if for any reason May 11th is not possible, there is an alternative, but far less convenient date on July 13th, so your second choice would be the week starting then.

The other two weeks of your holiday you would like to take during the fortnight commencing on June 8th. You have been selected to play for the county tennis team, and the County Championships take place at Eastbourne then. You would be bitterly disappointed if you couldn't take part, but some consolation would be to play in the Goldracket Junior Masters Championship at Weston-Super-Mare between August 3rd and 17th, and this would be your second choice. If neither of these were possible, you would go to Skegness for a fortnight from July 20th.

Your task is to negotiate with your colleagues to arrange a rota agreed by and convenient to all of you. This rota should be recorded on the form provided and handed to your tutor. You have 30 minutes to complete this task, otherwise your holidays will be arranged for you.

You can estimate your personal success by scoring 10 points for every one of your first choice weeks which is included in the rota, 6 points for a second choice, 3 points for a third choice, and 0 points if you accept a week you had not requested at all.

HOLIDAY ROTA
Wrightbite Confectionery Ltd

LEARNING
IN *ACTION*

HOLIDAY ROTA

WEEK BEGINNING		EMPLOYEE ON HOLIDAY
MAY	4	
	11	
	18	
	25	
JUNE	1	
	8	
	15	
	22	
	29	
JULY	6	
	13	
	20	
	27	
AUGUST	3	
	10	
	17	
	24	

© 1987   Roger Kirk   Basil Blackwell

PROMOTION

Objective	• to explore influencing and negotiating skills
Description	Five candidates are competing for two opportunities for promotion which have recently become available in a school. Each member of the group has the personal data of one of the candidates and seeks to influence the group accordingly
Target group	Staff, senior pupils
Organisation	Groups of 5 One/two tutors plus observers (The dynamics of this exercise can be altered by having groups of 6–7 with two participants working independently from the same briefing sheets)
Time required	1½ hours
Tutor skill	B (see page 17)
Location	Sufficient space for groups to work without disturbing each other
Materials	One briefing sheet per participant (Sheets are in sets of five, all different)

Tutor's notes

1. It is assumed that some work on influencing skills will have already been done

2. Form groups and issue briefing sheets. Indicate time allowed for discussion (*about 45 minutes*). If a decision has not been reached by then, the Governors will 'do their own thing' (*5 minutes*)

3. Groups work on the exercise (*45 minutes*)

4. General discussion during which participants should be asked to consider:

   • whether they influenced others; if so, whom? How?

   • whether they were influenced by others; if so, by whom? How?

   • what sort of arguments appeared most effective?

   • who in the group influenced most effectively? How?

   • how the group organised its discussion

   • how the group coped with the time constraint

   (*40 minutes*)

You are attending a meeting of the school's Senior Management Team. Two opportunities for promotion have become available, and the Team has met to decide what recommendations to make to the Governors about their allocation.

Your favourite candidate is Liz Swain. She is one of those young, involved teachers who will turn her hand to anything. She teaches English, History and RE and is a most enthusiastic and gifted form tutor, running Lower School discos and Christmas parties, looking after lost property, and undertaking the administrative arrangements for parents' evenings. She coaches two girls' hockey teams and helps with athletics. She assists with the school's social service unit, plays in the orchestra, has been on foreign visits and attends all staff functions. She was the first to volunteer to work on a pilot scheme for the introduction of profiling to the school.

Liz is only 25, but though she is an excellent teacher, with a 1st in History from Newcastle, she would never normally be considered for a promoted post as these in the past have been allocated rigidly to departments and she teaches across subject boundaries. You think it is high time this tradition was changed; it would be a real boost for the morale of younger members of staff, at a time of falling rolls and limited opportunities, for one of their members to be promoted. It would help Liz personally as well, as she has recently married and faces the expense of setting up her new home.

F

You are attending a meeting of the school's Senior Management Team. Two opportunities for promotion have become available, and the Team has met to decide what recommendations to make to the Governors about their allocation.

You feel strongly that one of these promoted posts should be awarded to Tom Haigh, at present on the basic scale. Tom is 26 years old, and came to the school to teach Spanish, the second foreign language, when he left Cambridge with a good honours degree. By any standard he is an outstanding teacher, popular with staff and pupils alike. As a result mainly of his enthusiasm and energy, the number of pupils opting for the subject and their success in public examinations has risen dramatically. The senior Spanish teacher retired at the end of last term, and will not be replaced because of falling rolls. You are fairly certain that if Tom were to leave as well, it would no longer be possible to offer a second foreign language at all.

Tom is fully committed to the school, takes part in all its activities, and has recently offered to undertake the production of the school play. This is all the more remarkable as he lives 20 miles away from the school. He is not one to make a fuss, let alone threats, but you know that the expense of travel, combined with a heavy mortgage and the fact that his wife no longer has a job as she is looking after their two young children, means that he is finding it very difficult to make ends meet.

You are attending a meeting of the school's Senior Management Team. Two opportunities for promotion have become available, and the Team has met to decide what recommendations to make to the Governors about their allocation.

You are very anxious that further promotion should be given to William Oakley, Head of Craft, Design and Technology. As head of this department he has been on a lower scale than the heads of English, Maths, Science, Languages and Humanities, and in the present climate you find this absurd. The impression given to outsiders that Technology is less important than these other subjects is little short of disgraceful, and you know that the subject adviser has urged this point on the Head and Governors in the past.

William, who is 52, has served the school loyally for over 20 years. During that time the subject has risen from being a 'Cinderella' undertaken only by the least-able academically, to one which is popular with academic pupils, and in which they get some of the best examination results in the Authority. Results in the 'Young Engineer for Britain' competition have also been noteworthy, with at least one finalist in three of the last five years.

Raising William to this new level would be a popular move with the other staff, as he is a greatly liked and respected colleague. He was Chairman of the Staff Committee for many years, and has served two terms as a Staff Governor.

You are attending a meeting of the school's Senior Management Team. Two opportunities for promotion have become available, and the Team has met to decide what recommendations to make to the Governors about their allocation.

You personally support the case of Samantha Tedder. She is a married woman in her mid-thirties with two children, who came out of industry five years ago to establish Electronics at the school. This she has done with signal efficiency and success. She has introduced a Computer Appreciation course, which is part of the core curriculum; Control Technology at GCSE level; and Electronics at both GCSE and 'A' level. There is a flourishing electronics club for pupils of all ages. The school's reputation in the electronics field is among the best in the Authority. It is certainly a draw for parents, and many other schools have been to see what we are doing.

Samantha is somewhat of a 'loner', being seen little in the staffroom, and known to have an abrasive style and sarcastic tongue at times. However, she has voluntarily written a programme for the school's timetable and has helped transfer school procedures and records on to the computer.

It would be a tragedy if the school were to lose Samantha, but at present she is only on the basic scale. She has certainly been 'approached' by other schools, and you know she has been to the Head to 'discuss her future'. You are fairly certain she would stay if she were offered a promoted post.

You are attending a meeting of the school's Senior Management Team. Two opportunities for promotion have become available, and the Team has met to decide what recommendations to make to the Governors about their allocation.

You wish one of these promoted posts to go to Jane Brewis. She is at present a PE teacher on the basic scale, but it is intended to offer her a new position as Head of 5th Year. You consider this new post to be vital. In the past, 5th year pastoral problems have come under the supervision of the Head of Middle School (Years 3–5), but new factors have meant that there has been a vast increase in the problems manifesting themselves among 5th year pupils. These factors include very high youth umemployment in the area, tension between racial groups, and an upsurge of drug abuse among the young.

Jane is an ideal candidate for this post. She is firm, forceful and effective, but at the same time sympathetic and a trained counsellor. She is well known to parents through her long-standing membership of the PTA, and staff respect her skills, which they have seen regularly displayed in the staff development programme. She is in her early 40s and lives on her own, being divorced and childless. She is therefore happy to devote much of her energy to the school.

You feel it is essential for the credibility of this new appointment that it is a promoted post. What is more, Jane has her pride (and is a Union official) and is very unlikely to accept the post unless it involves some clear advancement.

REDEPLOYMENT

Objective • to explore the principles of negotiation

Description A three-handed negotiation exercise in which neighbouring schools attempt to resolve their staffing problems to their mutual satisfaction

Target group Staff, possibly 6th form

Organisation Three groups of 4–7; any surplus members can act as observers
One tutor can cope; two or three are better

Time required 2 hours

Tutor skill A (see page 17)

Location One room for plenary plus two other syndicate rooms
or
One room large enough for three groups to work with privacy

Materials One briefing sheet and one staffing requirements list per group.
(These sheets are different for each group)

Tutor's notes

1. Discuss with the group the principles of and prerequisites for a successful negotiation eg trust, openness, honesty etc. Ask the group to record them on a flip chart and leave this displayed in the room. (*10 minutes*)

2. Divide the group into three teams with 4–5 in each. Any surplus members can act as observers. Allocate one school to each group and give them the relevant briefing sheets. Send teams to planning areas. (*5 minute*)

3. Teams complete the negotiation exercise. (*15 minutes planning plus 45 minutes exercise*)

4. *Review* in school negotiation groups, followed by general review. The discussion is likely to revolve around two issues:

   a *The result of the negotiation*
   • who 'won'? How did they 'win'?
   • how closely were the principles and prerequisites identified on the flip chart adhered to?
   • what did it feel like—especially to 'win' or 'lose'?

   b *the mechanics of the negotiation*
   • how did the groups organise themselves?
   • what were their strategy and tactics?
   • did they stick to the plans they had made?
   • did all three schools negotiate in one area or in pairs?
   • if the latter, were these negotiations consecutive or concurrent?

   (*30–45 minutes*)

5. *Solution*
   Avon's Cross and Beecroft can score 42 points; Cardingham can score 47 points.

You are the Senior Management Team of Avon's Cross School, an 11–18 Comprehensive. Your LEA insists that as the number of pupils on roll falls, staff must be reduced in proportion. The LEA has now informed you that for the coming academic year your number of staff must be reduced by seven. Rather than declaring anyone redundant, it is allowing you to negotiate with your two neighbouring schools, Beecroft and Cardingham, to see if you can solve all your problems by mutual agreement over redeployment. It has made it quite clear that it will look particularly favourably on any school that can reach its staffing target in this way, while schools which are unsuccessful may be penalised. For instance they may not be allowed to fill vacancies which have arisen as a result of promotion, retirement etc.

Your degree of success will be estimated as follows:
For each surplus teacher redeployed—5 points
For each teacher required whom you can obtain—2 points

You have analysed your staffing requirements for the coming academic year and these are shown on the attached sheet. You now have to approach Beecroft and Cardingham Schools to see if you can reach a negotiated settlement which will satisfy your requirements.

Stage 1
With your colleagues in the Senior Management Team, plan your strategy and tactics for the negotiation (*30 minutes*)

Stage 2
Negotiation (*up to 45 minutes*)

Stage 3
Submit to your tutor a written agreement signed by all the schools involved

LEARNING
IN *ACTION*

Subject	Staff at present in post	Staff required next academic year (including vacancies resulting from promotion, retirement etc)
Art	3	3
Biology	4	4
Careers	1	1
Chemistry	2	3
Commerce	2	2
Craft, Design and Technology	6	5
English	6	7
French	3	4
German	2	2
Home Economics	2	3
Humanities	12	9
Latin	1	0
Mathematics	6	8
Music	1.5	1.5
Physical Education	5	4
Physics	4	3
Special Educational Needs	2	2

You are the Senior Management Team of Beecroft School, an 11–18 Comprehensive. Your LEA insists that as the number of pupils on roll falls, staff must be reduced in proportion. The LEA has now informed you that for the coming academic year your number of staff must be reduced by seven. Rather than declaring anyone redundant, it is allowing you to negotiate with your two neighbouring schools, Avon's Cross and Cardingham, to see if you can solve all your problems by mutual agreement over redeployment. It has made it quite clear that it will look particularly favourably on any school that can reach it staffing target in this way, while schools which are unsuccessful may be penalised. For instance they may not be allowed to fill vacancies which have arisen as a result of promotion, retirement etc.

Your degree of success will be estimated as follows:
For each surplus teacher redeployed—5 points
For each teacher required whom you can obtain—2 points

You have analysed your staffing requirements for the coming academic year and these are shown on the attached sheet. You now have to approach Avon's Cross and Cardingham Schools to see if you can reach a negotiated settlement which will satisfy your requirements.

Stage 1
With your colleagues in the Senior Management Team, plan your strategy and tactics for the negotiation (*30 minutes*)

Stage 2
Negotiation (*up to 45 minutes*)

Stage 3
Submit to your tutor a written agreement signed by all the schools involved

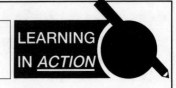

Subject	Staff at present in post	Staff required next academic year (including vacancies resulting from promotion, retirement etc)
Art	3	2
Biology	3	4
Careers	1	1
Chemistry	2	2
Commerce	2	1
Craft, Design and Technology	4	5
English	10	8
French	5	4
German	2	2
Home Economics	5	4
Humanities	7	8
Latin	0	1
Mathematics	7	8
Music	1.5	1.5
Physical Education	5	4
Physics	2	3
Special Educational Needs	2	2

You are the Senior Management Team of Cardingham School, an 11–18 Comprehensive. Your LEA insists that as the number of pupils on roll falls, staff must be reduced in proportion. The LEA has now informed you that for the coming academic year your number of staff must be reduced by seven. Rather than declaring anyone redundant, it is allowing you to negotiate with your two neighbouring schools, Avon's Cross and Beecroft to see if you can solve all your problems by mutual agreement over redeployment. It has made it quite clear that it will look particularly favourably on any school that can reach it staffing target in this way, while schools which are unsuccessful may be penalised. For instance they may not be allowed to fill vacancies which have arisen as a result of promotion, retirement etc.

Your degree of success will be estimated as follows:
For each surplus teacher redeployed—5 points
For each teacher required whom you can obtain—2 points

You have analysed your staffing requirements for the coming academic year and these are shown on the attached sheet. You now have to approach Avon's Cross and Beecroft Schools to see if you can reach a negotiated settlement which will satisfy your requirements.

Stage 1
With your colleagues in the Senior Management Team, plan your strategy and tactics for the negotiation (*30 minutes*)

Stage 2
Negotiation (*up to 45 minutes*)

Stage 3
Submit to your tutor a written agreement signed by all the schools involved

Subject	Staff at present in post	Staff required next academic year (including vacancies resulting from promotion, retirement etc)
Art	2	3
Biology	5	4
Careers	1	1
Chemistry	2	1
Commerce	2	2
Craft, Design and Technology	6	5
English	5	7
French	4	4
German	2	2
Home Economics	5	4
Humanities	8	9
Latin	1	0
Mathematics	10	8
Music	1.5	1.5
Physical Education	2	3
Physics	2	3
Special Educational Needs	2	2

YALE QUAY

Objective	• to improve problem and joint problem solving skills and influencing skills
Description	A complex problem-solving exercise with both an individual and a group element. The topic concerns a research expedition to a Pacific island, and the problem involves handling a mass of complicated logistical material over which an ethical choice is superimposed
Target group	Staff, 6th form, more able 5th formers

Organisation		
	Stage 1	Individual
	Stage 2	Groups of 5
	Stage 3	Plenary
	One tutor can manage, two are better	

Time required		
	Stage 1	Unlimited
	Stage 2	1–1½ hours
	Stage 3	15 minutes per group

Tutor skill	A (see page 17)
Location	Plenary room and group working areas with reasonable privacy
Materials	One set of briefing sheets per person

Tutor's notes

1. Give all participants a set of the briefing sheets. Allow considerable time for them to work on the problem on their own. (Ideal for private study, homework etc)

2. Form into groups of 5. Each group has to decide on an agreed solution. (*1–1½ hours*)

3. *Plenary* Each group in turn presents its solution. Tutor(s) challenge the findings—unless they are correct. (Points to challenge should be easy to identify from the solution sheet) (*15 minutes per group*)

4. *Review*
   Explore:
   a Any difficulties in individual problem solving
   b Any difficulties that arose in joint problem solving, especially behavioural matters.
   c Any pressure involved in defending the group solution, especially ethical considerations, eg
   • can the natives be left to die?
   • can Ichthyosaurus Golsonii be abandoned?
   • can the Sandhopper driver be forced to do without his rest?

5. *Solution*
   See *Tutor's Guide* on p 173.

You are a member of the University of Winchester Ecological Expedition, which is engaged in a survey of the Louisiade Archipelago in the Pacific Ocean. At present you are in charge of a sub-group of 11 people with the task of exploring the uninhabited and little-known Baxter Island (plan attached). You landed on the island with the necessary stores, transport and equipment some ten days ago, and are due to be picked up by your supply ship, SS *Santa Barbara*, tomorrow afternoon (October 3rd) at 14.45 hours at the main landing place, Yale Quay. The leader of the Expedition has emphasised how crucial it is for you to be at the rendezvous at the correct time. Because of unstable weather conditions, if the ship cannot take you off the island then, it may be another three months before she can return.

Your base camp is some 45 miles from Yale Quay and for the past 24 hours you have been dismantling it ready for tomorrow's departure. The only major items of equipment which you still have with you are the main medical supplies, including two collapsible stretchers, and all the remaining diesel fuel. The other members of your group with you are the technician, Joan Dixon, and your driver/cook, Josaia Rakoroi, who has been lent to the expedition by the chief of one of the nearer islands together with his vehicle, an Hiyota Sandhopper of considerable age.

Josaia is unpredictable both as cook and driver, and he and his vehicle are of equally uncertain temperament. Having heard of Western trade union practices, he insists on working to his 'rule book'. You have never actually seen this book, in fact you doubt whether it even exists, but you cannot risk arguing the point with him as he is the only person capable of driving the vehicle on which you depend. Among his 'rules' are an insistence that he must have four hours rest after every eight hours on duty. He is also adamant about the time required for preparing and loading his vehicle. If it is to carry a full load of passengers, he requires 30 minutes preparation time. If goods are to be carried, the time required to load or unload them depends on the number of people available to do the work. Two people can load or unload the vehicle in 40 minutes, four in 30 minutes, and six or more in only 20 minutes.

The Sandhopper itself is similar to a small transit van. It can carry one passenger together with the driver up front, and six further passengers or 1000 kg of goods (eg sufficient fuel for your group's small boat) in the rear. It also doubles as an ambulance and can accommodate the two collapsible stretchers, but as these constitute a 'load' if casualties are being carried, no other goods or passengers can be taken in the rear with them.

On the so-called roads on the island the Sandhopper can travel at an average of 30 mph unloaded and 25 mph loaded. In fact there are only three roads, the one that connects you with Yale Quay, and two others which branch out from your base camp. One of these leads to Copper Beach (30 miles to the North), the other to Needle Point (60 miles to the North East). These roads have been constructed for the Chief's hunting expeditions which visit the island two or three times a year. The rest of the island, consisting mainly of mountain, forest and maquis, is impassable except for a few rough tracks which permit travel on motor cycle, bicycle or foot only. Only one of these tracks has been of any use to you. It runs for 70 miles along the West coast of the island from Yale Quay to Copper Beach. This West coast is so rugged and has so many hidden rocks and reefs that no local boatman will risk his life by sailing along it. 30 miles along the track from Yale Quay are the awesome Ragged Rocks, and another track branches North East here to join the road junction at your base camp 20 miles away.

Of the remaining members of your party three are at Copper Beach: Professor Joan Carroll, the distinguished geologist; Dr Matthew Foster, the group's medical officer; and a research student, Kathy Anderson. They are engaged on a survey of the sand dunes, and have with them a serviceable bicycle which can be ridden at 10 mph on roads and 6 mph on tracks. The remaining five are at Yale Quay, preparing for tomorrow's departure. They are your two general handymen, Jim Lowe and Pete Berriman; two native bearers Alulau and Damu (nick-named 'Lulu' and 'Dammit'); and the skipper of your boat Kubu Volavola.

Like Josaia Rakoroi, Volavola is a 'character'. He obviously follows the same rule book as regards loading times, but he is a willing and diligent worker who certainly does not demand rest periods and who can get his boat ready for sailing in a remarkably rapid 30 minutes. The diesel-powered boat started life during the war as a US Navy liberty boat, hence its somewhat incongruous name *Madam Butterfly*. It can cruise at an average of 10 knots, can carry fuel for a 200 nautical mile journey (though its tanks are only half full at the present time) and can accommodate the same number of passengers or quantity of freight as the Sandhopper. Like the Sandhopper it is also in contact with your base camp by short wave radio. You have found *Madam Butterfly* a most useful means of transport between Yale Quay, Needle Point (70 nautical miles) and Copper Beach (a further 55 nautical miles beyond Needle Point).

Your group's only other means of transport, two ageing Triumph motor cycles, are also at Yale Quay. They are generally ridden by Jim Lowe and Pete Berriman and have proved surprisingly reliable, capable—without a passenger—of averaging 55 mph on roads and 40 mph on tracks. With a passenger or with an unloaded collapsible stretcher, which they have been adapted to take, they can still manage 45 mph on roads and 30 mph on tracks. They cannot, of course, carry passenger and stretcher at the same time.

Jim and Pete, as their description 'handymen' implies, are extremely versatile. They have limited training in first aid, and, on the one occasion on which you had an accident, proved remarkably competent stretcher bearers. As against their normal average walking pace of 3 mph, they could still average 2.5 mph with a loaded stretcher, provided they were relieved every 40 minutes. Without relief, they found they needed a rest of 15 minutes before they could go on again.

At 09.00 hours this morning (October 2nd) Kathy Anderson arrived at the base camp in a state of high excitement. Despite the fact that she was exhausted by riding her bicycle flat out for three hours, she couldn't wait to give you the message she had brought from Professor Carroll. In the early hours of the morning, during a search of the marsh grasses bordering the sand dunes at Copper Beach, the Professor had come across a living specimen of Ichthyosaurus Golsonii (see attached sheet), which had been assumed extinct for as much as a milion years. The previous evening the Professor had found skeletal remains permitting description of the internal features, but the unexpected discovery of a live specimen was, she guessed, easily the most significant zoological find of the century, filling an enormous gap in our knowledge. The animal had been placed in a tank filled with sea water, but if it was to survive, it must be got to the laboratory on SS *Santa Barbara* at the earliest possible opportunity. The tank could be transported either in the Sandhopper or on *Madam Butterfly* (it would require six people to load it), but the Professor would need to accompany it and the sea water would need changing every hour.

Twenty minutes later, when you had scarcely finished digesting this information, an exhausted and badly injured native staggered into your base camp. He told you that he had been fishing with four companions and foolishly they had sailed into the area of the Ragged Rocks. Their boat had been wrecked, two of his companions had been drowned, and he had had to leave the other two on the cliffs too badly hurt to move. From his description of their injuries, at the very least one had a smashed hip and the other a broken leg. He begged for your help in saving their lives.

You immediately tried to make contact by radio with *Madam Butterfly* and the members of your team at Yale Quay, but clearly the radio was out of order.

However, you have now made your plan of action and the time is 10.30 hours. What are you going to do?

LEARNING
IN *ACTION*

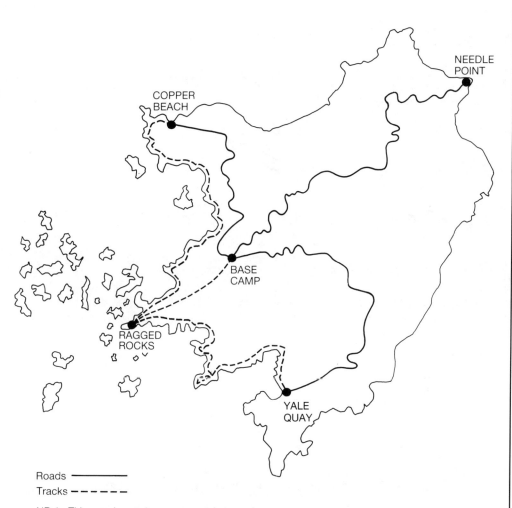

NEEDLE
POINT

COPPER
BEACH

BASE
CAMP

RAGGED
ROCKS

YALE
QUAY

Roads ————————

Tracks — — — — —

NB 1. This map is not drawn accurately to scale
    2. One nautical mile = 1.15 statutory miles

LEARNING
IN *ACTION*

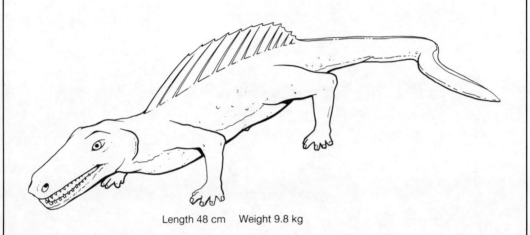

Length 48 cm   Weight 9.8 kg

Apparently a direct descendant of the first land-walking tetrapods, of which, until now, only a few fossils from the late Devonian/Permian boundary were known.

Despite such land-dwelling skeletal features as partial femoral head rotation, substantial limb girdle development, tetrapodal plantigrade galt and a tetrahedral scapulo-corocoid, it still retains the chondrichthian characters of a well-developed contraflowing gill system and rayed fins.

Other features that place it well within the early tetrapods are labyrinthodont teeth and characteristic 'Loxomatid' type keyhole orbits.

YALE QUAY
Tutor's guide

KEY	PERSONNEL		PLACES
L	Leader	BC	Base Camp
JR	Josaia Rakoroi	YQ	Yale Quay
JD	Joan Dixon	RR	Ragged Rocks
KA	Kathy Anderson	NP	Needle Point
KV	Kubu Volavola	CB	Copper Beach
JC	Professor Joan Carroll		
MF	Dr Matthew Foster		
JL	Jim Lowe		
PB	Pete Berriman		
A	Alulau		
D	Damu		

DATE/ TIME	SANDHOPPER	'MADAM BUTTERFLY'	MOTOR CYCLE/FOOT
Oct 2			
10.30	JR depart for YQ with instructions and stretchers and native who had brought message		
12.00	JR arrives YQ, delivers instructions and stretchers. Leaves native. Departs immediately for BC	KV prepares to sail	JL and PB depart for RR on motor cycles carrying stretchers
12.30		KV sails for NP	
13.00			JL and PB arrive RR, unload stretchers. JL stays with casualties. PB returns to YQ
13.30	JR arrives BC. Loads fuel with help of L, JD, and KA		
13.45			PB arrives YQ. Departs for RR carrying A
14.00	JR and KA depart for NP with fuel		
14.45			PB arrives RR. Leaves A. Returns to YQ

Time			
15.30			PB arrives YQ. Departs for RR carrying D
16.30			PB arrives RR. JL, PB, A and D depart for BC on foot with stretchers. M/cs abandoned
17.00	JR and KA arrive NP, start unloading fuel		
17.40	Finish unloading fuel. JR departs for CB via BC. Leaves KA at NP		
18.30	JR stops for rest		
19.30		KV arrives NP.: Loads fuel with KA	
20.10		Loading finished. KV and KA depart for CB	
22.30	JR resumes journey to CB. Picks up JD at BC en route		
Oct 3 00.40	JR and JD arrive CB. Wait for 'Madam Butterfly'		
01.40		KV and KA arrive CB, KV, KA, JR, JD, JC and MF load tank	
02.00	JR departs for BC with MF, JD and KA	KV and JC depart for YQ with tank	
03.00	JR arrives BC with MF, JD and KA		
03.15	JR, MF, JD, KA, JL, PB, A and D load stretchers		JL, PB, A and D arrive BC with stretchers
03.35	JR and MF depart for YQ with stretchers		
05.50	JR and MF arrive YQ with stretchers. Unload		

06.30	Unloading complete. JR rests		
10.30	JR departs for BC		
12.00	JR arrives BC. Loads L, JD, KA, JL, PB, A and D		
12.30	JR departs for YQ with L, JD, KA, JL, PB, A and D		
14.30		KV and JC arrive YQ with tank	
14.45	JR, L, JD, KA, JL, PB, A and D arrive YQ		
14.45	S S SANTA	BARBARA	ARRIVES

THE POWER GAME 1

Objective
- to examine the concepts of power and fear
- to open up the problem of bullying
- to improve co-operation, discussion and listening skills

Description
To explore individual concepts of power, participants are asked to place in rank order a number of power figures and then to compare their views. One of these figures is a bully, so the exercise is particularly useful as a means of opening up the subject of bullying

Target group
Years 1–3 (all abilities); can also be used with older pupils

Organisation
Groups of 4–5
One tutor; observers may be helpful

Time required
45 minutes (minimum)

Tutor skill
A (see page 17)

Location
Any room in which groups can work with reasonable privacy

Materials
One briefing sheet per pupil
(There are two versions of the briefing sheet: **A** and **B**. All members of one group should have the same sheet)

Tutor's notes

1. Divide the participants into groups of 4–5. Issue each participant with a briefing sheet. All members of a group should have the same briefing sheet (**A** or **B**); as far as possible there should be an equal number of groups tackling each sheet

2. Working individually, each participant draws up a ranking list.
   (*5 minutes*)

3. Groups negotiate a joint ranking list (*20 minutes minimum*)

4. *Review*
   Comparison of lists, especially **A** with **B**, and general discussion. The discussion should include (in simple terms):

   - the nature of power: why do you think *x* is more powerful than *y*?
   - the nature of fear: why are you more afraid of *x* than of *y*?
   - the relationship between power and fear
   - the misuse of power; the nature of the bully
   - reactions to the misuse of power
   - attitudes towards different power figures eg parents, police. . .
   - who exercised power (influence) in the various groups?

   (*20 minutes minimum*)

THE POWER GAME 1
Briefing sheet A

LEARNING
IN *ACTION*

1 Which of the following do you think has most power?
List them in order from 1 to 7

Your parents
Your headteacher
A magistrate
A bully
A member of parliament
The gang
A police officer

2 Discuss this list with the rest of your group.
Draw up a common list with which you all agree.

THE POWER GAME 1
Briefing sheet B

LEARNING
IN *ACTION*

1 Which of the following do you fear most?
List them in order from 1 to 7

Your parents
Your headteacher
A magistrate
A bully
A member of parliament
The gang
A police officer

2 Discuss this list with the rest of your group.
Draw up a common list with which you all agree.

THE POWER GAME 2

Objectives
- to explore the relationship between power and authority
- to examine legitimate and illegitimate types of influencing skills
- to improve co-operative discussion and listening skills

Description
A more advanced and intellectual examination of power, in which individuals define those attributes which they believe make a person powerful. They then explore power issues within the group itself and relate these to the list of attributes already established

Target group
6th form and staff

Organisation
Groups of 4–5
One tutor plus observers

Time required
1 hour (minimum)

Tutor skill
A (see page 17)

Location
Any room in which groups can work with reasonable privacy

Materials
One briefing sheet per participant
(Two versions are provided, each giving a slightly different perspective on the task)

Tutor's notes

1. Establish groups of 4–5. Issue each participant with a briefing sheet.

2. Working individually, each participant draws up a ranking list.

3. Groups negotiate a joint ranking list (*30 minutes*)

4. *Review*
Comparison of lists and general discussion. Points that should emerge will include:

- behaviour within the groups themselves. Which members of the group were most successful at getting their points of view accepted? Who had the power? How?

- possible means of power, eg material advantages; role/position; physical attributes; intellectual ability; verbal dexterity; manipulative skills. . .

- the relationship between force, power and authority

- misuse of power in our own community/school/college

(*25 minutes*)

1 List in rank order from 1 to 5 those attributes which in your view make a person powerful. (*5 minutes*)

2 Agree with your group a common list of such attributes, again ranking them from 1 to 5. (*30 minutes*)

THE POWER GAME 2
Briefing sheet

LEARNING
IN *ACTION*

1 List in order the five most powerful people in your life
(*5 minutes*)

2 *a* Compare your list with the others in your group and agree a general list between you.

   b Analyse the list to determine what makes people powerful.
(*30 minutes*)

VANDALS

Objectives	• to explore the problem of vandalism (This exercise can also be used as a consensus exercise to examine group behaviour and influencing skills)
Description	The exercise explores value systems and attitudes through the problem of vandalism. Participants are asked to identify the reactions they personally find most and least acceptable and to achieve consensus as a group
Target group	Years 1–5, 6th form
Organisation	Groups of 4–6 One tutor (plus observers if group behaviour is to be considered)
Time required	45 minutes–1 hour
Tutor skill	C (see page 17)
Location	Any room in which groups can work with reasonable privacy
Materials	One briefing sheet per pupil

Tutor's notes

1. Issue briefing sheets. Ask the pupils individually to read the newspaper report and comments carefully and to write down

   a the *three* comments with which they agree most closely

   b. the *one* comment with which they disagree most strongly

   (*10 minutes*)

2. Divide the class into groups of 4–6. Ask the groups to discuss and if possible agree

   a the *three* comments with which they agree most closely

   b the *one* comment with which they disagree most strongly

   (*25 minutes*)

3. *Review*
   Each group reports its decision. Groups compare these and identify any common feelings about the problem of vandalism.
   (The review can also include comments on:
   • group behaviour.
   • influencing skills—which members were most successful at 'selling' their views?)
   (*20 minutes*)

A From the *Shabbington Reporter.*

SCHOOL UNDER SIEGE

For the third time in ten days vandals struck at Downtown Road Primary School last night. Already reeling after the theft of over £1,000 worth of audio-visual and computer equipment early last week, and the attempted arson at the Caretaker's house at the week-end, distraught staff and pupils arrived at the school today to find trees smashed, plants uprooted, windows broken and the building daubed with yellow paint. Headteacher Kate Bird (56) said: 'We are all deeply distressed. What are they trying to do to us? It is the children who are suffering most.' Chief Inspector Nick Lock of West Anglia Constabulary said: 'Someone must have seen or heard something. It is up to the public to help us track down these vicious vandals'.

B Comments made after reading the above report:

   1 So many pupils fail at school, it's hardly surprising if they don't value it. *Educational psychologist*

   2 Discipline isn't what it was in my day. *Chief Constable*

   3 I enjoy the sound of breaking glass. *Unemployed teenager*

   4 If you haven't any self-respect, why the hell should you respect other people? *Outward Bound organiser*

   5 If schools look shabby and neglected, this sort of thing is bound to happen. Why should children care if apparently the authorities don't? *Headteacher*

   6 Teacher's don't have authority any more. It's all that industrial action. *Parent*

   7 Most of these vandals come from very disturbed backgrounds. It isn't really their fault. *Vicar*

   8 Bring back the birch. *Member of Parliament*

   9 Parents don't seem to care where their children are or what they are doing. *Probation Officer*

   10 This must be tackled by education. Children must be taught the importance of respecting other people and their property. *Librarian*

   11 School buildings are not adequately protected against this sort of thing. *Crime Prevention Officer*

12 What do they want all that expensive equipment for anyway? *Senior Citizen*

13 It needs someone to stand up to these vandals and to tell them that there is no place for them. *Newspaper editor*

14 It is wrong to blame the schools. We all share responsibility for putting things right. *Professor of Sociology*

15 The devil still has many things for idle hands to do. *Magistrate*

16 The present generation of youngsters is disillusioned. What has society to offer them? *Youth worker*

17 I cannot understand what enjoyment they get out of this. *School caretaker*

18 If children plant the trees themselves, they are far less likely to be pulled up or damaged. *School Buildings Inspector*

19 Potential vandals should be identified much earlier and educated in special units. *Secondary School teacher*

20 This never happened when I was at school. Things have got far too permissive. *Chairman of County Council*

21 It's only a minority. The majority of our pupils today are highly responsible. *National Charity Organiser*

Appendix: Application of the Exercises

	Communication	Consensus	Group behaviour	Influencing	Information retrieval	Negotiation	Observation	Planning	Presentation	Priorities	Problem solving	Values
Boom! Boom!			•				•	•				
Capitation committee		•		•		•					•	
Classroom corridor	•		•									
Combined operations	•		•									
Evening out				•		•				•		
Family business							•	•	•			•
First things first			•					•	•	•		
Furniture removers												
Holiday rota	•	•		•							•	
Horse of the year	•					•					•	
Islands in the sun					•							
Jordan Homes Ltd.			•	•		•	•	•	•		•	
Little boxes			•			•	•	•			•	
News-stand			•	•			•	•			•	
Orange market				•		•			•			
Promotion	•		•				•					
Raffle	•			•								
Ranking 1 & 2												
Rawhide			•			•	•	•			•	
Redeployment												
Reservations												
Scramble												
Survivors			•			•	•	•		•	•	
The Arkbuckle Bell	•									•	•	
The go-between	•		•	•								
The power game 1				•				•				•
The power game 2				•				•				•
Vandals		•		•								
Visitors								•				
Yale Quay				•							•	

Bibliography

Adair, John (1983), *Effective Leadership*, Pan

Argyris C and Schon D A (1978), *Organisational Learning: A Theory of Action Perspectives*, Addison-Wesley

Brandes, Donna and Ginnis, Paul (1986), *A guide to student-centred learning*, Blackwell

Kolb, D A (1983), *Experiential learning: Experience as the source of learning and development*, Prentice-Hall

Revans R W (1983), *ABC of Action learning*, Chartwell-Bratt

Revans R W (1980), *Action learning*, Blond and Briggs